Create Yourself in Business

Use Your Own Unique Brand to Inspire Trust and Attract Ideal Clients

Amy Rosner, PhD

ISBN-10: 1721215654
ISBN-13: 978-1721215652

Dedication

This book is dedicated to Duke and Daisy, my fuzzy posse, for the therapy they give me every day.

Contents

Foreword

"Creating Yourself," that is what life is all about! This book gives you an easy-to-follow map to get out of your own way and do that!

I first read this encouraging and eye-opening book when it was under its original title, "Create Yourself As A Hypnotherapist". I had just left a 16-year career in the corporate world where I had gained a wealth of knowledge and experience, but where I had also lost myself.

My business was in its infancy stages of life, and to say I wasn't nervous and stressed would be a lie. I met my now trusted and dear friend, Dr. Amy, at a networking meeting. Her passion to help others get out of their own way resonated with me instantly, specifically, because I am ALWAYS in my own way. LOL!

After hearing a bit more about what she did through hypnotherapy, I scheduled a session. I had done hypnotherapy before, so I was already a believer and craved the Kool-Aid. However, sessions with Dr. Amy were different. I was amazed at how quickly the hurdles were knocked down, but even more amazed that they were no longer stacked in the corner for the next race. They were just gone.

At the end of one of our initial sessions, she told me about the first version of her book. Even though I was working to become a Personal Chef, I knew I needed to read, "Create Yourself As A Hypnotherapist". I got home after my session that day, and devoured the book, page by page. I still look back at my notes written on the specified note pages, in the margins, and squeezed into the body copy because I couldn't wait long enough to flip to a notes page to write down the "ah ha's" that continued to occur as I read.

The words and lessons in the first version of this book are still with me today. One of my favorite quotes is, "Surround yourself with smart, supportive, positive people, because you just got on an emotional roller coaster that's on its way up a big incline at the moment."

I recently buckled in for my next roller coaster ride. I'm excited to break in my sharpened #2 pencils as I devour each page in "Create Yourself In Business" from the top of my next first incline!

Jo Jackson
Author of *Cut the Carbs, Keep the Flavor!*
Owner, J2h Eat Enterprises, LLC
San Tan Valley, AZ, June 2018

Acknowledgements

I want to send a huge thank-you to Eric for being my rock, my love, supporting me in every conceivable way, and making this hypnotherapy gig possible. Big thanks also to my parents for their unwavering faith and helpful advice, even when they thought I was nuts. To my mentors and teachers, thank you thank you thank you for the guidance to get me started on my way. And to my friends, colleagues and clients - you are the best! Thank you all for being such integral and enjoyable parts of my continuing education and growth on this journey.

Life is a work of art created by
the one who lives it.

Introduction

At age 46 I found myself jobless with a house and two dogs to support. I've started over in new careers before, but this time was scary.

I was a college professor and psychology researcher for many years, but I felt that I was dying a slow death when I thought about teaching the same classes every semester for the next 30 years. I wanted to feel that I was really helping people, and I just didn't get that from research. I had no desire to go into psychotherapy, which never appealed to me. I didn't like seeing people as broken, and I had a hard time seeing how I could know what was best for someone.

I wound up having a life-changing experience about ten years ago. I was exhibiting some of my artwork at a show in Phoenix, and a new life coach fell in love with a couple of my prints. She offered a year of coaching in exchange for them. I was a cold, creepy brain researcher and feeling very smug, so I didn't think I would get anything out of such a warm, fuzzy pursuit. But I'm game for just about anything and agreed. Surprisingly, I wound up making some fantastic discoveries about myself and made some very healthy and needed changes in my life.

I loved and believed in it so much, I couldn't stop thinking about how wonderful it would be to give that kind of experience to others. What a rewarding way to make a living! But I would have to go through training and open a business and find clients and...and...and...do many things I've never seriously considered doing. I had always worked for institutions. That was my comfort zone, so I started doing more and more coaching work for institutions.

But when I found myself without an institution, I was at a complete loss. Several of the people closest to me encouraged me to take the plunge and open a private practice as a life coach. It was who I really was, they said. The were right, but I was petrified. I did it, though. Got some great training, a good phone and a business license, and I was off and running.

Something was still missing, though. My attention and memory research kept coming back to me and insisting that there was a faster, more effective way to get my clients past the frustrating blocks that take so long to address when talking to a conscious mind. I was driven to help people get over such blocks, and I felt that hypnotherapy was the missing piece of the puzzle. As soon as I came to that realization, everything fell into place quickly and easily, as though the universe had been waiting for me to take off in that direction. I learned the best techniques available, and from the first time I practiced hypnotherapy I felt completely at home doing it.

Combined with coaching, I found hypnotherapy to be a great way to help people get more control of their minds and bodies, reprogram emotional blocks and get on with their lives. Talk about immediate gratification! There's nothing better than to see a client who was in terrible pain at the beginning of our session leave my office smiling, feeling comfortable and hopeful. Not every session is that dramatic, of course, but it happens remarkably often. I've helped many clients get rid of negative emotion and limiting beliefs that have held them back, sometimes for decades, and shown them techniques for keeping negative reprogramming from occurring, and it feels amazing. It's the work I've always wanted to do and was born to do, but I just didn't know it until recently.

I knew it would be difficult to grow a business into a profitable enterprise, and I knew it would take time. Possibly a very long time. I've never been one to ask for help from others, and being completely self-sufficient and successful is a part of my core identity. I did not want to be a burden to my loved ones, so I figured I needed to work as hard as I could to shorten that time as much as possible. To that end, I would wake up as early as 5:30 in the morning to call in to coach training, then spend the rest of the day in hypnotherapy training. And that whole time I was fitting everything I was learning into my attention and memory researcher mindset, into the work I had done as a college professor. It all fell into place beautifully. I knew just how I wanted to utilize the techniques I was learning and I was beyond excited! While others in my training program were going out, I was giving free sessions over Skype to a good friend back home who agreed to be my guinea pig. I wanted to get my practice sessions out of the way while still in training so that I could hit the ground running with a full-time practice as soon as I got home and found an office.

My first full month as a hypnotherapist I made a lot more money than I thought I would - actually enough to live on! It was touch-and-go for the next couple of months, then I had another big month. Then another, and another. By my sixth month in my office I started wondering when the well would dry up. For the whole first year I wondered when the well would dry up, and it never did. It just got better. I exceeded my income goal for that first year. I was apparently doing something right.

I received a little business training in my coaching program and a little more in my hypnotherapy program. I needed a lot more, though. All in all, I felt like I was starting off with very little knowledge of how to have a private practice. I read a lot and asked a lot of people a lot of questions. I changed the way I did everything at least a couple of times. What I wound up realizing was that a hypnotherapy business (at least the way I envision it) isn't like any other business out there and that I was plowing my own path, finding my own way. Many of the ideas that helped me most went completely against what I had been told over and over were good business practices, and many best business practices produced more disappointing results than doing things in my own, unique way.

Practitioners like myself are in an interesting situation. We have private sessions with clients but don't diagnose or treat diseases or disorders. It's a cash-only business and we have to find our own clients, rather than being funneled clients from insurance companies. So many of us go the used car salesman route with guerrilla marketing and even prey on each other. How, I wondered, do I create a reputable practice without shoving my products and services down people's throats? One of my friends told me he had to change his email address after giving it to a very famous and successful coach. I did not want to be one of those coaches, but I wanted to be successful.

My idea of success was helping as many people as I could, utilizing personal sessions as well as passive income streams such as product sales that got my message out to many more people than I would able to see in my office. So I surrounded myself with professionals I respected and admired, and I learned all I could from them. I even found that sometimes they wound up learning from me, as well! I made alliances with many great practitioners and other businesspeople, and I'm proud of the way I built and continue to grow my business.

A number of my contemporaries have wanted to pick my brain about how I have had the success I've had almost right from the start, and a few of my fellow hypnotherapy school graduates and trainers have strongly encouraged me to write a book about what I did and how I did it to help other new hypnotherapists who may find the information helpful. So I published *Create Yourself as a Hypnotherapist* in 2015, which was my own personal experience and ideas in my own words. Since then many entrepreneurs in other rapport-based professions have read the book and found it invaluable, and many of them have encouraged me to publish a new version of the book that is focused on rapport-based businesses in general, not just hypnotherapists. So here is that new and updated version. In these pages I don't pretend to know what's best for anyone, even for myself at times, but I share what has and has not worked for me as I've traveled down this road.

I'm still learning and will continue to do so for as long as my business exists, I expect. I have a great love for what I do and how my business has taken off. It's still a fledgeling but its wings are flapping hard and it's staying aloft and actually getting somewhere. And best of all, I feel proud and comfortable about the way I'm doing business. A couple of hypnotherapists have asked me why I published this book, because giving away all of my secrets might mean more competition for me. I disagree. There is no competition, because I am the only hypnotherapist like me. I am qualitatively different from all others and will resonate with different people. I want us all to be successful as the unique individuals that we are. If anything I've learned, implemented or created may help others survive and thrive in their businesses, I will be very happy to have shared it. I wish all of us - and our clients - great success.

To that end, in the following chapters I have addressed the major lessons I've learned above and beyond the nuts and bolts I received in my training programs and the additional seminars, webinars and workshops I've experienced, and I have provided some activities for anyone looking to get started from scratch or move in what might be a new and more profitable and/or enjoyable direction. I want to give you the benefit of my experience. This doesn't mean I don't think you should pursue other avenues. To the contrary - go for it! Some sales approaches, etc., that didn't work for me might work for you. Everything is worth a try. We're all different and will find success in slightly different ways.

At its heart, my business philosophy is about developing ourselves as people and putting ourselves out there in the public domain in a good way as our true, creative selves, as role models and educators, spreading our messages of hope and help and happiness for all.

Chapter 1
POKING ALIENS

The most frightening day of my life was the day I decided to start my own business.

I have never considered myself business owner material. Economics was the only class I ever dropped in college. I started my professional life in academia, where the academics were pitted against the administrators, who ate their young. This is, of course, an unfair misrepresentation of academic administrators, but it is one I formed and found more and more evidence for (because I was subconsciously looking for it, of course) as I worked as a college professor year after year.

I have never been attracted to the idea of making more and more money to have more and more stuff, and I grew to see those who valued this idea as morally destitute. I saw successful businesspeople as those who have ruined others' lives as they trampled their way to the top of the financial hierarchy so that they could have more stuff than anyone else. They were damaged and overcompensating for weaknesses, lack of love, or lack of empathy. They were evil. They were so far beyond my comprehension that they may as well have been aliens.

This is the realization that was reflected back to me by Dr. Irene Lebedies, life coach extraordinaire. Right after I completed my hypnotherapy training and certification (during which I did some serious reprogramming of these limiting beliefs), I started sessions with Irene. I knew I was now in the "business owner" category, and it did not sit well with me. I had no idea what to do or how to do it, and I did not want to own it. I hated the corporate world. I was overwhelmed, adrift on a boat that I did not have any idea how to pilot. I would have to identify myself as a business owner and be comfortable in that role if I were to have any hope of having a successful business. Irene, who has an amusing way of making ideas real and meaningful, pointed out that it was as if I was poking at an evil alien whenever I talked about doing business. A business owner was a life form about which I had no understanding, and I would poke at it every so often to learn a little more about it. That's exactly what it felt like!

Then my boyfriend provided the next big realization along my journey into business owner. He said that there may be evil aliens, but there are also good aliens. Two distinct species of alien! I didn't have to try to identify with the evil aliens, after all. I could poke at the good aliens instead and release the idea that I had to find a way to identify with an entity that I knew I could never become (the bad aliens).

This idea instantly resonated with me I think in part because my dad was a successful businessman and has always been one of the most ethical, well-adjusted people I've ever known. He instilled in me a reverence for nature and helping those around me, in leaving a place in better shape than I found it. He's the kind of guy who always makes me want to be a better person. He would definitely fall into the "good alien" category. He had a lot of good advice for me as I formulated my business, but I realized quickly that only some of that advice would work for what I was beginning to see as my off-the-wall, non traditional industry. I wasn't selling widgets. My business was dependent on the rapport and trust I inspired in my clients. I gathered up his and other good aliens' advice and teachings like a neurotic squirrel gathering nuts, not sure what would help and what wouldn't but being open to and grateful (desperate, more like) for it all.

I had started going to local business networking meetings (which is where I met Dr. Irene). I reflected on the wonderful people I met at those meetings and realized that I knew many business owners who were good people. They were principled, lived by their values and genuinely cared about their clients. They lived the lives they wanted to live and were happy. I could be one of those good aliens. After just a bit more poking, they were no longer aliens at all, they were my fellow business owners and I was proud to be part of their tribe.

I had created myself as an entrepreneur who did business in accordance with my values and priorities. I could call myself a business owner and smile, proud of that huge emotional accomplishment. I have a much healthier view of businesspeople now and don't concern myself with the ones who are still evil aliens to me. I don't identify myself with them at all. This was a significant growth experience for me, as it is for many others I've known. Every one of my fellow entrepreneurs who has been unsuccessful at making this shift has been understandably unsuccessful in business.

This is just one of many limiting beliefs that a new or struggling business owner may have. Another very common one is having a scarcity mentality, which makes them more competitive than cooperative with their contemporaries, desperate, overzealous or non selective with clients, or makes them believe that for some reason they should not make more than a certain amount of money (they don't deserve it, they won't be good people, etc.). It's all subconscious, of course, but our limiting beliefs about money, capability and success, to name a few, can negatively impact our success in our businesses. The sooner we discover and reprogram those limiting beliefs, the sooner and more rapidly we can grow our businesses, because *we are our businesses*.

I realized quickly that having a hypnotherapy practice meant I automatically have two full-time jobs. One job is doing hypnotherapy. The other job is running a business. Any ideas or beliefs I have that keep me from giving both of those jobs equal attention and enthusiasm at all times will keep me from being successful. Professional growth first requires personal growth. My business grows from me, from my values and philosophies and motivations.

GET A BUSINESS COACH

... preferably one who will exchange services with you. You'll get a better understanding of yourself as a business owner and how to develop as such, and you'll get a new referral source.

Your Coach's Name: _____

At first I was so overwhelmed with getting a business up and running that all I could do was try to get the minutiae covered. What should my business cards look like? Should I make brochures or rack cards? What exactly *is* a rack card?! The thought of a detailed and well thought out purpose for my practice made my head explode. I knew I was attracted to this profession and it felt right. I knew I wanted to help people and I had a valuable service to offer, and that was enough for me at the beginning. I needed to get the nuts and bolts figured out first and be open for business so I could start making money so I could *stay* in business helping people.

I wasn't even sure who my clients would be. I talked to many hypnotherapists who started out thinking they would specialize in one thing and wound up specializing in something else because of the clients they wound up attracting. I knew that my clients would choose me, and it was my job to give them whatever they wanted that I had to offer. I decided that I would put myself out there as authentically as I could and let my clients tell me what they wanted from me.

As it turned out, my specialty has more to do with my background than the types of changes my clients want to make. People attracted to my background and philosophical orientation have more trust in my services. My background is in basic science, in psychology and biology, specifically the neuroscience of attention and memory, as well as in creativity and art. I get many clients who identify more with scientific and innovative orientations. They tend to be logical and practical. People who are skeptical about hypnotherapy but open-minded enough to give it a fair try do very well as my clients. They tend to be adults (though I have a great time with children too), roughly half female and half male. They are intellectual and hard-working. I tend not to attract as many people who are more metaphysical or spiritual in their orientations, though I have a few clients like this and they do very well, too. Just because we specialize doesn't mean we have to reject anyone as a client (though we always have that option, of course, and should definitely use it when appropriate).

So there are many different ways to specialize, and specialize we all should. I heard this emphatically from both coaching and hypnotherapy trainers, and I completely agree with them. However, I do not agree that we should have our specialties completely worked out when we start our businesses. I think we should let our clients decide for us. And the only way our clients' choice of specialty will work for us is if we put ourselves out to the public in an absolutely authentic way. If you're not a kid person, for example, don't say you work with kids (you still can, just don't advertise it). If you're an environmentalist and the most important element of your services for you is teaching people to mobilize their natural healing processes, make this known and have a natural feel to your office, your appearance and your website. If you have wrestled with a particular type of limitation that you got over using your type of service, there's your hook - others with the same issue will see you as a kindred spirit.

We attract what we put out there, so if we put ourselves out there honestly and passionately, we'll get more of our ideal clients (who will refer others like them) and our specialty will reveal itself over time - certainly within the first year. In other words, while I encourage you to specialize, I encourage you to let it happen naturally, organically, and modify it as your business develops. Be yourself to the world, emphasizing what's most important to you about your service, and you'll attract your ideal clients without thinking or strategizing about it.

EXERCISE

Make a list of your qualities, values, interests and preferences (e.g., love kids, women's empowerment, spiritual growth, etc.). These are qualities that define you as a person; don't think about how to define yourself in your business just yet (we'll get to that later).

_____

_____

_____

_____

_____

_____

_____

_____

_____

_____

_____

_____

_____

_____

NOTES

NOTES

NOTES

NOTES

Chapter 2
I GOTTA BE ME!

Hypnotherapy requires relaxation. I don't know about you, but I can't do that in a suit...or even in closed-toed shoes. This presented a bit of an issue for me, because I was initially trying to emulate my mentors in all ways, including dress. They dressed professionally, with heels and pantyhose. I found myself having a bit of an identity crisis.

I decided to do my own thing and make it part of my branding. Once I worked through this, I relaxed and began to see this "be yourself" concept at work in other businesses, big and small. Dutch Bros Coffee is a great example of this. It's still a family-run business that presents in a non business way, in that all of the employees wear whatever ultra-casual attire they want and are genuinely friendly and accommodating to all of their patrons. You don't feel like a stranger at a Dutch Bros, you feel like part of their family. Turns out, family is very important to the owner. One of the two brothers who owned the company passed away from ALS years ago, and every year the company has a big charity drive to raise money for ALS research. The company is still in the family, and the remaining brother looks, sounds and acts like he just put his surf board away and has beer for everyone. Check out his appearance on the television show Undercover Boss. He's down to earth and not the least bit pretentious, and that is the way his company is. He is his company, and he makes sure his values, beliefs and style are represented proudly. People happily wait in line for 30 minutes or more at a Dutch Bros not just for the great coffee (I can honestly say I've never had anything but great coffee there, and I go there all the time - I can't say the same for Starbucks), but because there is a personal relationship, a rapport, between them and the company, via the wonderful, vibrant folks working there. One visit there and you know, you feel, what that company is all about.

Another smaller company example that I noticed is a one-woman operation that is growing like crazy - Dr. Sara Solomon. She's a dentist and fitness spokesperson who has turned her personal health and fitness journey into a thriving training company. She is big into social media and puts out videos often, and she lets herself just be herself. She's off-the-wall and makes mistakes and shows cat bloopers and is really amusing. Watch just one of her videos and you feel like you know her as a person. She instills trust. Even if you, as I did, watch her videos and think to youself, "This is a train wreck and I can't look away", she draws you in and, as nuts as she is, gives her viewers a lot of fantastic and research-backed information (not bro-science) about nutrition and fitness.

These examples have two things in common. First, they have no gimmick, but rather trade on their authenticity, their transparency, which instills trust in their services. Second, they really deliver. They do great work and deliver it in their own non traditionally business ways. These are the companies I feel good about doing business with, because they resonate with me deep inside, at the value and trust level.

Instilling that resonance of value and trust is so important for a rapport-based business. In fact, I might even go so far as to say it is everything if the business owner has a personal stake in the business beyond making money. My business is about making a difference one client, one workshop participant, one book reader and one CD listener at a time. I realized that I had to truly be myself and let my values shine through in all that I do in order to resonate with my ideal clients. I had to be at one with my work, and therefore relaxed, for my clients and potential clients to resonate with and be attracted to my brand of relaxation.

It's a positive snowball. Being relaxed not only helps my clients relax, it also makes it more comfortable for me to do my work and really be myself to have better relationships with my clients, which leads to better results. It all comes down to what my clients believe. They have to believe in themselves (or at least be willing to entertain the idea), and they have to believe in me.

There are many ways to let the real me shine through and give clients and prospective clients a good feel for who I am and what I'm about - and whether they would be comfortable working with me. The first thing I had to do was to stop emulating others and get a unique vision of myself as a professional. This vision included everything from my appearance and demeanor to my office and website. It is all a reflection of me, of my practice, and it has to fit me and make me comfortable. Clients comfortable with my vision will be more likely to have good, successful experiences with me and will be my ideal clients and refer more ideal clients to me.

I am a beach bum at heart. Dressing as my most comfortable self would be decidedly unprofessional by anyone's standards. I'd look like I work at Dutch Bros, which I'm totally down with but felt was a bit casual for a hypnotherapist. I spent some time finding an Amy uniform that would resonate with me as looking casual but professional. I settled on a long comfy skirt, plain tee shirt and sandals. I also wear my own homemade jewelry. I look like I should be in the Bahamas, but I look professional. My demeanor is relaxed, confident, fun and professional because that's how I feel. I come across as authentic and transparent to others, because I am. All cards are on the table and what you see is what you get. Honesty. Trust. Complete lack of judgement.

What do I get in return? Clients who feel comfortable enough to open up to me about some very personal information that they have difficulty discussing with anyone.

If you enjoy working in a more corporate environment, you and your clients may feel more comfortable if you wear suits. You, your work environment, your clients - everything about your business - should all have the same basic style so everyone is comfortable.

Speaking of environment, I realized that my office appearance would also be very important - another reflection of me. Some hypnotherapists, particularly those who focus on medical support, only make house calls. This makes sense for clients who have difficulty leaving home. For other clients, however, I believe that an office is a must. And I don't mean a home office where you're looking into the kitchen during meetings and passing bedrooms on the way to the bathroom. I remember how uncomfortable I felt going to a professional's home office for sessions years ago, even though the services I received were top-notch. When I tell people I'm a hypnotherapist, very often the first question I'm asked is if I have an office and where is it. Having an actual office in a nice office building when I started out put me in a completely different tier of professionals, and only four full-priced sessions each month paid for it. Eventually I realized my dream of having an office suite at home with a separate outside entrance off of a beautiful courtyard and a professional feel (this is actually quite common for higher-level mental health professionals - if it would not fly as professional in your field, don't do it). My clients love it, they get optional dog therapy at no extra charge, and I can't beat the commute.

I had several things to consider when choosing an office space. The first, of course, was price. I wanted to spend as little as possible for a nice, professional looking space that included a receptionist to greet my clients (which I discovered were called "executive suites"). With my current office I pay a higher mortgage but that extra money is a great investment. I also wanted to be in a more central location than where I lived when I started my business. I'm in a big metro area and lived in the *extreme* southeast.

Driving a bit farther to my office in a more central location could have made a difference in clients' perceptions of whether their drive will be worth it. My office is not in the middle of the city - far from it - but it's near a freeway and easy enough to get to that my clients drive in from all areas of town, often from over an hour away.

When I started out, I was able to get my (almost) dream office at my (almost) dream price. Yes, it *is* possible, at least temporarily. Pick a spot you like, ask for a deal and you might want to lock in a long-term lease (because - be ready! - everything changes). Consider the restaurants and other businesses nearby, the vibe there, how easy the owners are to work with and the reliability and professionalism of the receptionists, if there are any. Are there conference rooms where you can have workshops? A kitchen? Do they cost extra? Can you make copies there so you don't have to have a copier, paper and ink in your office, and will they keep your office clean? How reliable are the wifi and cellular reception in your actual office space? Pick a place that won't nickel and dime you to death and that gives you a great deal on a great space that works for you and makes you feel comfortable and professional.

I was amazed at the logistics that we hypnotherapists have to work out within our office spaces - more so than some other professionals. Windows are not our friends, though we can learn to live with them. Neither is general office noise. I once put a big, light-colored painting on a wall to give an impression of a window so my clients wouldn't feel like they were in a windowless room, even though they were. I also use a free white noise website (SimplyNoise.com) to minimize the impact of office noise on my clients, and I have a sign, "In Session, Quiet Please" that I hang on my door. The feeling in my office is one of a cozy, comfortable living room.

I always have a sitting area on one side of my office (in my current office I have a separate waiting room) that is inviting and allows new and potential clients to learn more about my services without having to sit in the recliner. There is a lot of misinformation out there about hypnotherapy, and some folks who come in for consultations are very nervous about sitting in the recliner - sometimes to the point of leaning up against the wall farthest from it! I have three good-sized upholstered armless chairs around a wicker storage box that I use as a coffee table. I want my clients to feel comfortable, including larger individuals (many of

 my clients come to me for help with weight loss). Consider your potential clients and why they're thinking about using your services when you decorate your office.

I shopped around for good deals on nice furniture because I didn't want clients to see cheap furniture and think that was all I could afford. Nothing says "I'm barely squeaking by" quite like hard chairs and ugly metal file cabinets (unless you're an accountant, then you get a pass on cheap furniture, as it just makes you look like you practice what you preach).

I have professional books as well as more personal tokens on my bookshelves, including thank-you cards and gifts from clients. Because I use a coaching paradigm, not psychotherapy, I have a more personal relationship with my clients. We coaches want our clients to know that we're right there with them, running their course with them, supporting them. We don't maintain the rigid distance that therapists do. To that end, a few personal items and plants in my office help increase my clients' (and my) relaxation and perhaps even trust. It's one more thing that helps them connect with me on a deeper level. And to increase relaxation even more, natural scenes have been shown to reduce stress, so I keep a natural theme in my office. Lots of trees and birds (not sure how the bird thing happened, it just worked out that way).

I even have a mala tree to display the mala bracelets that I make for my clients. When I teach a client how to do self-hypnosis, I let them choose a mala from the mala tree and teach them how to use it to deliver suggestions to themselves. Whenever I go to networking meetings or other get-togethers now I always see several people with my malas on their wrists or hanging from their purses or backpacks, which is very cool and makes me feel like I've really made a meaningful impression on them. It's something special I do for my clients just because it's fun for me as a jewelry designer and it's not something everyone else does. It's become part of my brand and sets me apart. And every time they look at their malas, they think of me and the positive changes they've made in themselves. In this way it is a very special marketing tool. Think about what you can do for your clients that would really come from your heart and soul - that's your brand, and a material expression of it that you give them is part of your marketing. Please note that I am not talking about putting your logo on a pen or coffee mug! Anybody can do that, and it may actually cheapen your business image. You want something truly special and unique to you.

Starting out with a new practice, I had more time to spend than money. I did my research and really put some thought into every item I put into my office. Could I have spent less? Yes, but not much, and there would be a big difference in the feel of the place. I wanted it to feel like...well...me.

I wanted my logo to feel like me, too. I designed one that has special meaning for me, and that I thought looked cool. When I was a kid, I used to sign my name with a butterfly at the end. I've always identified with butterflies, as I've always been an independent risk-taker, often referred to as a free spirit. The butterfly also represents the transformational processes of my services. But as much as I liked it, feedback is golden. Don't send anything to press without getting feedback first.

Amy Rosner, PhD

Why have a logo at all? Because it makes me look professional, like a real business. It's on every business card, brochure, ad, sign, web page, DVD, CD and book that I produce. It ties everything together. Just keep in mind that a logo doesn't have to be an image. It can be just your name or business name in a particular font, if you like.

That was another thing I changed, my business name. I used to have a cool, touchy-feely coaching business name because that was the convention in my field, but the more people I met the more I realized that they had a hard enough time remembering *my* name, much less my business name. So I rebranded with just my name. I pretty much have been trying to go through life anonymously, so it felt weird and uncomfortable (and still does), but it works much better for me. I am my business and my business is me, so it just makes sense. If my business grows into some big entity, I can rebrand with a corporate umbrella name, but to start I was most concerned with building my brand focused on my own unique interaction with my clients.

I also wanted my website to feel like me. I wanted people to understand me when they first saw my site, as I knew that it would be many potential clients' first experience and impression of me. I enjoy doing all of my own web work, but if you pay someone else to do it, make sure it feels like *you*, not the web designer. Always remember that rapport is the most important ingredient for success with our clients, so they have to see your personality and energy when they visit your site. Don't try so hard to make it look professional that it has none of your personality shining through.

That's what happened with a coach friend of mine. She used a professional looking template and filled it out with professional text and photos, and it was very nice. But it didn't have any of her big, wonderful personality! She has since changed her text to sound more like her when she talks to people and added photos that show her personality and how she interacts with people. Now I see her when I look at her website, and others who don't know her can get a better understanding of who she is and whether her style resonates with them.

I see my website as my extended office and, with automation, a (almost) free employee. It represents me. It has to feel like me, be easy to use and work flawlessly. It also has to be scalable. As my business grew, I quickly realized that I had to totally redo my site on a new platform because the first one did not allow the automation, search engine optimization, plugins, etc., that would save me more and more time and money down the road. I am my business - just me, doing almost everything. I can't spend any more time than necessary on my website. Setting it up with my mature, successful business in mind, not the 2-client operation it started out as, made it scalable so that it grew (and continues to grow) with my business. It's important to realize that a website is never done. My site is always changing. It's the visual manifestation of my business vision, and it changes as my vision changes (more on that later).

All this said, the biggest selling point for your business is you. If you come across as a happy, healthy, well-adjusted person, then potential clients will be attracted to that because they want that, too. At first I was hesitant to put my picture on my business cards because I thought it was too much of a realtor thing - that's stereotypically high-pressure sales, and I didn't want to give that impression. Then one day I was having lunch with a couple of entrepreneur friends, and one of them, who has had many years of great success, held up my rack card (yes, I found out what they are), pointed to my picture and said, "This is why people make appointments with you. You look happy and relaxed and like you've got it all together, and they want that for themselves." At that moment I decided I would always have my picture on my promotional materials.

It doesn't have to be a professional picture, either. My first one was taken by a sculptor friend who was kind enough to meet me for coffee one day at my favorite local hangout and she took about a hundred pictures of me with her phone. We decided on the one we liked best, and I used it until just recently when I cut my hair and started wearing glasses (now I use a selfie that I edited myself, and it looks great). You can get a fabulous head shot from a professional photographer, and sometimes at a great price. Just make sure that you look like you and not staged or artificial. The look on your face will tell them all they need to know. After all, what's a more appealing look on someone's face than having fun with a friend? Buy 'em a cup of coffee and maybe even a muffin for their help (don't forget to write it off as a business expense!). Your relaxation and happiness will shine through and make you a billboard for your business, for the positive life changes that can be made with your services.

CREATE A VISION BOARD (PAPER OR DIGITAL)

Include your logo, a picture of you, pictures of clothing, office furniture & accessories, office buildings, the area of town you would like to set up shop, website ideas, and anything else that strikes your fancy and helps you get a full view of your business. Look at it as a whole collection and replace anything that doesn't make you feel comfortable or professional.

Last but not least, a big part of being you is showing others who you really are inside. Don't be afraid of standing up for your values, beliefs and opinions, as long as you have no ill intent. Use your voice and influence for what your believe will make your profession, the world, or even just your little corner of it, a better place. I went into my new role as a business owner believing I had to try to make everyone happy and remain neutral in all things so as not to offend anyone. I was attracting all different clients, including some I really didn't want to have.

Then I heard some business trainers recommend actually creating a controversy to get attention. I couldn't imagine doing that! Their rationnale was that nobody talks about the folks who stay quiet and seem to be okay with everything, never making any waves. Needless to say, I disagree with that strategy. It's too evil alien for me, and it's not honest. They have a good point, though, that people who remain neutral and okay with everything do not engender trust, because nobody knows who those folks are. They are not being honest, either. So while creating a controversy or getting other types of negative attention may get you talked about, it may not be the best way to get business. However, putting yourself out there in a good way with common sense and an attitude of helping others will help others get to know the real you, they know you care enough to try to make a positive difference, and they will know that you say what you mean and they can therefore count on you to be honest with them. The truth is that you never know what part of you will inspire trust in your clients, so just be unapologetically you and let it roll. One of my clients told me that when I said the word "shit" during our consultation, she knew she could really trust me. You just never know. Being you creates trust with the people you want as clients.

EXERCISE

What things, beliefs, events or activities make you relaxed and happy? As in the last exercise, don't think about relating them to your practice just yet. Just have a brain dump here with no limits or filters.

_____

_____

_____

_____

_____

_____

_____

_____

_____

_____

_____

_____

_____

_____

_____

_____

Now, compare what you just wrote with your vision board. Are they in synch? How can you incorporate more of what you came up with in the exercise into your vision board? Does the picture of an office chair on your board make you feel comfortable? If your idea of a comfortable chair is really not doable for an office, how can you compromise so that the chair you have is comfortable yet works for your office (size, professional feel, etc.)?

Do you paint? Weave baskets? Add them to your office decor, use them in brochures and other promotional materials - find ways to add more of you to your business. When people feel like they're getting to know you just by looking at the photographs on your walls, your book collection or some meaningful personal trinkets, they'll feel more comfortable with you and with the possibility of working with you. You will have inspired trust by opening yourself up to them even more and in different ways.

Analyze every item on your vision board, comparing them all to the things that make you relaxed and happy, and add a version of everything on your happy/relaxed list to your vision board. Incorporate everything you can. Are you into feng shui? Use a bagua map to organize and decorate your office space. Love going to spas? Incorporate that feel into your vision board. You can even make up a general office floor plan if that helps you visualize. In other words, make your professional space one of personal comfort and good vibes in your own unique style.

NOTES

NOTES

NOTES

NOTES

Chapter 3
THE BIG VISION

I got the look and feel of the superficial, physical, logistical part of my business figured out, which really felt good because I felt like for the first time since starting my business I had control over something and had really built something. As I was getting my elevator pitch ironed out and determining what makes me unique and why people should give my services a shot, however, I realized that I had a lot more work to do.

I have never been comfortable singing my own praises. I've always felt that I'm the epitome of the average person. My accomplishments are things anyone could do if they wanted to. That attitude, even if it were true, won't sell sessions. A fellow business owner took me aside at one of my first networking meetings and told me I really had to let everyone know about my accomplishments and strengths (thanks, Bryan McClure from Primerica, who became my friend and financial advisor). I earned my degrees, my skills, my wisdom, and I should not be shy in sharing that information. That's the stuff people wanted to know about me, he said. Every hypnotherapist does similar work, so I needed to let people know how I'm unique.

This made sense to me and I went back through the bio on my website and my elevator speech and made sure that I gave people a more complete story of me and what I brought to the table that was different from other hypnotherapists. We all have different backgrounds, skills, interests and knowledge, and we should celebrate that! We don't want to all be the same. Different hypnotherapists will appeal to different people with different personalities and ideals who want to accomplish different things. That's the way it should be. "That's why," my grandmother Mimi used to say, "they make chocolate and vanilla."

The more I worked on ways to present myself as the unique professional that I am, the better I felt about what I had to offer my clients. The real me was breaking through the mold I had in my head of the perfect hypnotherapist, into which I had been trying to shoehorn myself. I found myself wanting to start projects that incorporated hypnotherapy with my previous research background to come up with new ways of helping people. The more I let my fun, creative spirit out to play, the more I realized I had to offer.

So I decided to throw caution to the wind and just be me. If I felt like writing a book about a new perspective on living mindfully, I would do so, and I would do it my way. The more I integrated my previous experience and knowledge with my new hypnotherapy knowledge and skills, the more excited I became about how unique I really was as a professional. That excitement started to shine through with every interaction I had, and I found myself with more and more clients, product sales and speaking engagements.

It was clear to me that my prior background and knowledge were extremely important. They made me who I am, made me unique. They gave me an angle, a niche, and made me more marketable. So what I needed to get crystal clear was my angle, my message, my big vision. I kept thinking about a business vision as an abstract schema of some kind that I found difficult to wrap by head around.

Then one day it hit me - my website is my business vision. It's the visual representation of everything I want for my practice and for my clients. As I clarified my philosophy and what I wanted people to know about me, and as I completed fun projects, I changed my website to reflect these updates. It kept me organized in my thinking, too. I could see whether my offerings made sense as a collection or if other products or services could be offered to fill in any holes and help everything make more sense together. (Not to mention, frequent, regular changes increase a website's SEO, or search engine optimization, helping more clients find you.)

If you're a visual person but not inclined to do your own website, you might want to consider making a vision board. Or you can create a mind map or flow chart or anything else that resonates with you. Just as you did with the day-to-day operational elements of your business in the last chapter, put together a collection of elements of your BIG VISION. Include everything that is on your website - your background, accomplishments, orientation, philosophy, interests, services, products, workshops, etc. What unique keywords best describe you as a professional? What is your hottest undeniable benefit to clients? What are your dreams for your business in ten years?

Once I incorporated my background and interests into my big vision, I was almost overwhelmed by the rush of creative ideas I had for workshops, products and other directions in which I could develop my business. My vision kept me grounded and was a reality check. It was great to let my ideas run wild and add to my vision, but at the end of the day I wanted to have a vision that made sense and was not overwhelming. I wanted to feel comfortable with the products and services I offered and the way in which I offered them. I thought more and more about what I was doing and how I was doing it, what was working for me and what wasn't. Anything I was doing just because I thought I should be doing it got thrown out the window. I got to really thinking about my approach to my hypnotherapy sessions and wound up with my own process for helping my clients get what they really wanted from my service.

I took to beginning each session with coaching, and I noticed an interesting pattern. When I asked my clients how things had been going since our last session, they would talk about some positive changes but would often focus on the negative. After asking a few more questions to get a more complete picture, however, we realized that the negative wasn't really so negative; in fact, they often showed improvement but hadn't realized it until I asked them about it. They also often forgot about some of the positive experiences until pressed to remember them. They just weren't paying attention to the more positive stuff, focusing instead on the negative issues with which they've had trouble for so long and which have in some cases defined them. Once they realized all of the good things that happened in their lives since our last session, they smiled more, their faces relaxed, their stress was visibly reduced and they were excited to continue in a positive direction.

I understood from this epiphany that using hypnotherapy to help people release the stress, negative emotion and limiting beliefs that do not serve them is just the first step toward what they're really after. Incorporating my background, interests and current research into this picture, I came up with a system that I feel we all tend to follow in order to have lives that are optimally satisfying. I believe that we need to **release** what doesn't serve us, **grow** by gaining all the knowledge and experience we can about what we want instead, **create** our own unique style, system or process for doing it, and then put our unique work out there in the world to **inspire** others (and ourselves).

As my hypnotherapy sessions focused on the release step of my four-step system, I began to offer workshops and products to keep my clients progressing through all of these steps after they had successfully completed their sessions. I had their complete success in mind, not just the completion of the first step. I wanted them to have lives they enjoyed and to never again think, "There's got to be more to life than this."

This realization was a life-changer for me. By not pigeon-holing myself into just helping them with that first step and letting my creativity and passion run wild, by giving myself permission to be free to be me, I had so much more to offer! And because I was so excited about what I was offering, I had so much fun giving talks to as many groups as possible to spread the good word. And I realized that I had unknowingly completed my own *release-grow-create-inspire* journey with starting up my business and had come out thriving!

I made wonderful alliances with professionals in other disciplines who had similar views about how to do what's in the best interest of our clients, and I started getting referrals from psychotherapists, coaches, massage therapists, chiropractors, doctors and others who were impressed with my philosophy and enthusiasm. I wasn't trying to sell my services to any of them, I was just having fun talking about my passion and learning all I could about what they did and how they did it - and how they could help my clients. They gave me lots of great ideas about how I might be able to grow my business. Not all of those ideas worked for me, but I was off and running - and with more potentially tasty nuts to add to my stash!

Now when I think about my elevator pitch I have a very different approach. It's easy to give my unique perspective and what I really help my clients achieve rather than giving a generic description of what a hypnotherapist does. It's no longer about the session, it's about long-term results. Those who find that what I say about my practice resonates with them become clients - my ideal clients - and have great results. And they tell others about me. Those who do not resonate with my approach would not become clients, which was a good thing, because they would most likely be better served by a different professional with a different orientation or philosophy. My practice grew organically from this point on, and I have continued to grow in my own unique way, offering something truly special and feeling amazingly good about doing my thing my way to help people the best way I can.

Make Your Big Vision Visual

Find a way to make your business vision a visual reality as your website, a vision board, or perhaps a flow chart - whatever works for you to really see the big picture. Look at it almost every day and make any changes, whether big or small, that make it feel more comfortable and exciting to you.

EXERCISE

Compare your big vision to the qualities, values, etc., that you listed in the exercise in Chapter 1. Are those qualities represented in your big vision somehow? What's missing? Modify your Big Vision board, website, or other visual so that those qualities that best define you are clearly represented. In the case of your website, doing this ensures that you are communicating your values, interests, etc., to anyone interested in learning more about you.

NOTES

NOTES

NOTES

NOTES

Chapter 4
ALONE ON MY ISLAND

So I just finished hypnotherapy school and I'm sitting alone in my comfortable office with my degrees and certificates, trees and birds, a developing business vision and very few appointments wondering what to do with myself. I just signed a year lease and got to move in early, so I have six weeks to come up with the $500 rent payment for next month. That was my financial goal for my first partial month, just coming up with my first rent payment. If I hadn't sold a pair of $19 earrings at the local yoga studio, I wouldn't have made it. It was that close.

I start to hyperventilate and wonder what I was thinking getting into an office lease. That's where my support system really kicked in, and in multiple ways. Surround yourself with smart, supportive, positive people, because you just got on an emotional roller coaster that's on its way up a big incline at the moment! I've successfully tackled some pretty lofty goals in my life, but I frequently panicked throughout my first year in business, especially at the very beginning. If it weren't for the amazing and unwavering support of my boyfriend and dogs, family and friends, I would have been in much worse shape.

(Dogs can be surprisingly good sounding boards, by the way. They listen intently, their ears go up when you say exciting things and they give you the paw when you're in need of calming down or changing perspective. They can help you work out some of the more off-the-wall ideas and feelings you have so that the humans in your life don't think you're nuts.)

I knew it would take some time to make what I considered a success of this gig, but I was impatient and put a lot of pressure on myself. My boyfriend talked me down off the ledge and back to reality on many occasions. I also realized that regardless of my support system, making my business work was totally up to me. I had to have faith in myself. So whenever the panic would rear its ugly head, I would remember my first lesson from coach training and channel that negative energy into positive action toward my goal (thanks to my mentor coach, David Krueger, MD). And I had to make peace with the fact that I wouldn't really be able to start understanding my patterns of business until after the first year, when I was no longer throwing every marketing gimmick at the wall to see what would stick.

I also realized that I would not make it as a business without other entrepreneurs' support. I could not think of my business as an island. Referral sources are essential, as are service professionals that make sense to use for your business. I remember reading an interview with some ridiculously successful businessman who said that my goal as a business owner should be to fire myself from as many jobs in my business as possible. I forget now who that was, but he was absolutely correct (well, almost - more on that later).

Right away I understood the value of firing myself from accounting and bookkeeping work. I would rather be strung up by my toes than do that work. I don't want to learn the ins and outs of it, either. Seriously, it's all I can do to keep up with my mileage. It would take time that I would be happier spending doing hypnotherapy. One session a month more than covers what I pay a professional for those services. As I would spend more than one session's worth of time on that dreaded work, it actually saves me money to use someone who really knows what she's doing. She's also another contact and possible referral source for me.

I also understood the importance of having legal advice at my fingertips. What recourse do you have when someone just won't pay you for a session? I had no idea. Every time something of a legal nature came up, I wanted advice from someone in the know. I received a letter from a lawyer one day asking for session notes at the request of the client. I thought about just sending them, but I didn't know what ramifications there might be from doing that. I signed up with LegalShield early on and have asked a lawyer every legal question I've had. It's really paid off. In the case of the session notes, it turned out that I could have potentially opened up a can of liability worms had I sent the documents without a release form signed by the client! Half of a session each month pays for legal and identity theft protection for myself, my business and my boyfriend. And I got another referral source and client out of the deal. I met the awesome representative, Kimberly Bruns, at a networking meeting and we became friends and part of each other's support network.

This is no small thing - you'll really want and need the emotional support of your fellow entrepreneurs on a regular basis. They understand this rollercoaster better than anyone and they need you as much as you need them. You are not alone! I don't care how much of an introvert you think you are, all entrepreneurs need each other's support to have the most fun on the coaster and let go of the tension by screaming with others on the same ride.

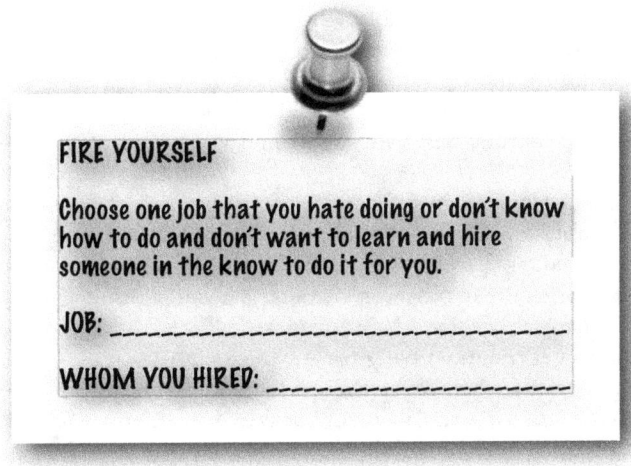

FIRE YOURSELF

Choose one job that you hate doing or don't know how to do and don't want to learn and hire someone in the know to do it for you.

JOB: _____

WHOM YOU HIRED: _____

So now I have a couple of other expenses and still no clients except a couple of barters with fellow networking group members (they're great to barter with, by the way, because they are quick to give you testimonials, which bring you more clients who will pay for your services). How do I fill my practice with paying clients? I'm not a "go drum up business" type of person. I'm an introvert whose definition of hell is mingling.

You may be thinking that social media would be the perfect place to grow my business. I can stay home by myself and get on the computer when I want to in my pajamas. As appealing as that is to me, it was not the answer for me. For one thing, there are many individual differences in platform preference. You have to find your tribe on the right platform and be completely committed to that being your way of connecting to others frequently and meaningfully. This takes a lot more time and energy than you might expect, and if you don't have the right personality shining from your posts on that platform, you won't be successful. This approach can come in handy for increasing long-distance business for some people, but for those of us focused on local business it's a sorry substitute for face-to-face interaction.

I can honestly say that I started to build my practice by going to inexpensive local business networking groups, getting to know other entrepreneurs and giving free talks to as many of them as possible. First I joined my local chamber of commerce and went to an educational event they had. Everyone at those events wants you to get to know about them and their business - they want you as a possible referral source and/or client. They know they have to reciprocate, so they want to get to know you and your business, too.

One bubbly woman (who became another good friend) at that first chamber event told me about a networking group that she really enjoyed, so I went to the next one of their meetings and got to know more great business owners. The networking group had several chapters nearby, so I went to all of them as often as possible to get the most bang for my buck, and I got on all of their speaker agendas. Whenever there was a speaker cancellation and there was a call for a replacement speaker, I was always the first one to volunteer. Whenever I didn't have a session scheduled I'd go to a networking meeting to promote my business.

Self-confidence is everything. Even though I hated giving elevator speeches at those meetings, I knew I had something epic to offer. I knew I had a great background and an effective set of tools. I helped my fellow hypnotherapy students in practice sessions when I was just learning, so I knew that I would help others, too. I made peace with the fact that I was new to this field and would not be perfect right out of the gate, but knowing I would help people made me confident and enthusiastic to get as many folks into my office as possible. I knew they would receive value from my services and that I would get more comfortable and effective with every session. I didn't have a catchy tag line, but I honestly conversed with the individuals in the group to connect with them on a personal level, and they remembered and trusted me for that.

Now when I give elevator speeches at networking meetings, I change it up every time, giving them interesting bits of information that applies to them or someone they know. For example, one time I told everyone that hugs increase the hormone oxytocin, which increases our empathy and that researchers say we should give/get 8 hugs every day to increase this hormone and have better relationships. That caught their attention so well that they nicknamed me "the Hug Doctor" at that meeting. Years later, some of them still call me that, and it's a conversation starter with others who hear it. I became memorable. And by giving them new information, the same people may see me at many different meetings but pay attention to me because they hear something different and interesting about what I do every time I give my pitch. Instead of saying the same, well rehearsed bit every time and seeing their eyes glaze over, I keep them awake and learning more about me. I still hate giving elevator speeches, but it's much easier now and I have more fun with them because I see them as educational public service announcements, not sales pitches.

I learned early on, and it's been reinforced over and over since then, that I get more clients when I just have fun talking about my work than when I try to sell it. I read all I could (that was free online) back then about marketing my business and wanted to make sure I was doing everything I should be doing the way I should be doing it to have a successful business. I heard over and over that no matter what business you have, your main job is sales. I understand what they mean, but this view did not work for me at all. People can smell your desperation when you're in sales mode. Nobody wants to be sold. So no matter how few clients I had at the time, I distanced myself from being a salesperson. Salesperson is just too much in the evil alien category for me. And when you use the "tried and true" sales techniques with other businesspeople, they immediately recognize what you're doing and put up their guard, because they read all of the free online marking stuff, too.

Whenever I felt desperate for sales, I just made myself relax, got to know more people and focused on learning from them and letting my enthusiasm for my work come out naturally. With that focus, I had more people ask me to do one-on-one meetings with them, and those people very often became clients and referral sources.

I would encourage you to experience different networking groups. All of the ones I've ever known have let guests come to at least one meeting free. Go to as many as you can and at least get in front of some different people. When you're first getting started, it's all about letting as many people as possible know that you're around and doing what you're doing.

If you decide to continue to go to a group's meetings, there are expensive groups and not-so-expensive groups. Join the best groups you can afford to join. What are the best groups? For me they were the relationship-based groups, not the lead-based groups. I've received much business from networking groups, but only from people I've gotten to know who also became clients. Unfortunately, not everyone is looking for a hypnotherapist. We're not like dentists or dry cleaners. They have to be interested in learning more about what we do and how it might benefit them - and they often want a referral from someone who has experienced us first-hand. Leads groups require their members to make a certain number of referrals each week for other members of the group, whether they've used their services or not. I've never had someone make an appointment because someone from a leads group referred them to me. Ever. All of my referrals have come from clients.

Leads don't really help hypnotherapists much because the potential client has to be interested in hypnotherapy in the first place, to understand what it really is all about compared with the scary but entertaining mind control it's touted as at fairs and Vegas shows, and he or she has to be ready to go for it, to put in whatever effort it takes and make a change. Selling doesn't work for us. If we get a client because he wasn't all that interested but we convinced him to give hypnotherapy a shot, the chances of him achieving good results are not so good.

Our best potential clients are those who take the step to get to know more about us - and they're more likely to do that if we're not trying to get their business. Once there is a relationship there, they know whether they feel comfortable and want to take a journey into change with us. They'll find us when they're ready. We just have to do all we can to be visible and accessible to them when they're ready. Don't think that if you get a lot of leads from a meeting, you'll get more business. People will tell you it's a numbers game, and you need more leads to get more business, but it just doesn't happen that way if you're not selling widgets - at least it didn't for me. Hang out with folks with whom you want to have relationships and/or who may be good referral sources for you.

Your referral sources may surprise you. Take note that not all of your colleagues in related fields will send you business. I was amazed how many of my fellow holistic wellness practitioners were not willing to refer their clients to me. One of them, who really liked me personally and respected me professionally, actually told me point blank, "I will never refer a client to you, ever." She said she was sure the client would never return to her after working with me.

There is a great deal of competition in the holistic wellness fields, as in many other fields, though there's really no reason for it as far as I'm concerned. There's plenty of business for people who are good at what they do and stick around. Look for practitioners who are specialized and actually have a scope of practice. If one of your colleagues is not willing to turn away any potential clients, that person is not likely to refer anyone to you or anyone else.

Anyone who claims to be able to help anyone with anything is not a referral source, nor is a someone who does a dozen different things. I know a number of people who have added lots of additional services into their repertoire because they weren't getting enough business from their main service(s). It's one thing to add essential oil sales to a massage therapy practice (that makes complete sense and may be a very good idea), but when that person also adds hypnotherapy, coaching and crystal healing, look out! This is someone who is desperate for business and will not be likely to send business your way.

Look for specialists in complementary fields. For me, those include counselors and other psychotherapists (different specialties), doctors, chiropractors, massage therapists, physical trainers - the list is practically endless - *who realize the value of and adhere to their scope of practice*. I want a legion of really great professionals to whom I feel confident referring my clients who need help outside my scope of practice. I've also made a lot of good friends this way, with people I respect professionally. You won't only meet these folks at networking meetings, but it's a good place to start.

ATTEND A NETWORKING MEETING

Find a networking group to try out, perhaps at Meetup.com. Attend a meeting and get to know as many people as you can who might be good referral sources for you.

Group:_____

Time/Date/Place:_____

One of the first and best professional alliances I made was with networking coach Jacque Zoccoli, with whom I instantly bonded and who was kind enough to take me under her wing and to some networking events with her. I had no idea what I would get out of these or any other events, but I made a rule for myself that if I had the opportunity to go to an event that might help my business, I would go. Some of the events that I thought would be complete wastes of time wound up paying off for me, so I tried not to judge and just go. I made sure to go to all of Jacque's events, too, and pretty soon I was pretty much her sidekick, the Ed McMahon to her Johnny Carson (I'm dating myself with this example, aren't I?). We had, and still have, lots of fun at her events, and I learn something new and helpful every time.

I lucked out, because networking coaches are a rare breed and desperately needed, especially for those of us who don't have staff and do all of the work ourselves. We have to maximize our productivity as much as possible. Her information about how to make connections, the different types of connections I should make, and what to do with the deluge of business cards I collected helped me get more business growth out of those activities and saved me a lot of time. It was tough for me, being the introvert that I am. My idea of networking is going to the event, finding the bar and enjoying a glass of wine at a table, talking to whomever stops by to say hi, then going home. Jacque made it much easier and more productive for me. I no longer have to attend so many networking events, but it's always good to stay in front of people, to get out there and stay connected and to continue forming and nurturing professional relationships, my support network.

As you get established, I would encourage you to spend more time with people who are successful (by your definition) and can help you be more successful. Sit down one-on-one with someone going through the same challenges you are, who understands, and with whom you can work on possible solutions. Find small mastermind groups composed of other business owners who can give you different and helpful perspectives from their different types of businesses. Raise the level at which your business mojo is vibrating.

That said, continue to enjoy groups you may feel you have outgrown professionally, because you may have made some great relationships and can feel good about being part of their support network. It's good to keep growing as a business owner and moving to groups that are composed of a higher caliber of entrepreneur, but it's also good to pay it forward by sticking with lower-level groups when you're past the rookie stage and can help other rookies grow and succeed.

EXERCISE

List all of the jobs you do in your business and how much time they take (per day, week - whatever makes sense to you). Put an asterisk (*) next to those that someone else could do for you. For example, you have to do your sessions, but perhaps someone else could do your social media posts or newsletters. The jobs that others can do for you that take up the most time are the ones you'll probably want to start thinking about how you can farm out to a person or service so that you can spend more time doing the things only you can do, like sessions, going to networking meetings, writing books, making CDs, etc.

_____

_____

_____

_____

_____

_____

_____

_____

_____

_____

_____

_____

_____

NOTES

NOTES

NOTES

NOTES

Chapter 5
EDUCATE, DON'T SELL

The first thing we all learn when we become hypnotherapists is that almost nobody understands what we really do. When we ask people what they know about hypnosis or hypnotherapy, we almost always hear something about clucking like a chicken. You may have similar misunderstandings in your field of expertise (probably minus the chicken).

It became clear to me early on that my primary mission had to be to educate everyone I possibly could. Learning the truth about what I do makes people much more interested in experiencing it, and, let's face it, it's just a fun topic to discuss with people. For those interested in sessions, it's imperative that they understand that what they will experience is not therapy but rather an educational process that helps them take more control over their minds and bodies. *They* hypnotize themselves, *they* have all of the answers, *they* do the reprogramming - they do all of the heavy lifting. I am just their guide and instructor toward self-empowerment.

Seeing myself as an educator first and foremost was a liberating thing for me. When I was in teacher mode I was not in salesperson mode. I was in my element, as I am a teacher at heart and by training. I don't want to see myself as trying to "fix" anyone. I teach people how to make changes in their attention and memory to manifest whatever changes they want to see in their lives. This is my approach to my practice, as I spent years as an attention and memory researcher. But you don't have to be a teacher or former teacher to become a teacher of empowerment. People don't want to be sold, but they do want to be educated if they'll get something out of it. So my attitude is to teach as many people as possible how to have more control of their minds and bodies and always give them something free. Perhaps you teach your audience how to do a simple progressive relaxation technique. You made no money for yourself, but you just made the world a slightly better place. Maybe they'll pay it forward, and when any of those folks want help making a change or know anyone else who does, they'll look you up. Why? Because you've given them something and asked for nothing. You've instilled trust that you are out for their best interest.

It's a great learning experience to go to networking meetings. Listening to others give talks to discuss their businesses and how they try to get your interest really lets you see how different approaches go over. I learned a lot about what I wanted to do and what I did not want to do. I've experienced the hard sell from many of my colleagues, and I decided that I did not want to take that approach. You can also tell which people buy into the idea that no matter what your business is, you're always selling. They come across differently than those who just educate you about their services. They do not instill that same level of trust, because they're more concerned about a slick sales pitch than giving you helpful information - they're in it for themselves and you'll benefit, too. Totally different feel, totally different rapport.

I read all about how to give talks that lead the audience to purchase your product or service at the end. I've tried various versions of this and have seen it done many, many times. For some people this is a great technique. I'm clearly not one of those people. I cannot successfully orchestrate my talks to have the audience buy my stuff at the end. It's not me, and my audience can tell.

I have to go in to any talk with just a bare-bones outline in mind. I am very relaxed, low-key, encourage audience questions and participation, and I take the talk in whatever direction they want to go. I've learned that when I do that, they get more excited about what I have to say and get more out of it. I never know what my audience wants - it depends on many factors of which I am never privy (who they are, what's important to them, etc.). I just have an idea to start myself off, such as sticking to New Year's resolutions for a talk delivered in January or February, give them some interesting and perhaps controversial ideas, see where the discussion takes the group, then when my time's about up I circle back to the original topic to wrap up. At the end I let them know how they can put their interests into action at their convenience with the products and services that I offer, which can be found on my website, and that they can get more information by getting in touch with me anytime. I encourage them to take advantage of my free one-on-one consultations to learn more, no strings attached. I offer my products and services to help people, not to make sales (though I have to make money to stay in business, of course - more on this later), and that's the attitude with which I present them.

The hard-sell and sneaky-sell techniques that I see all over the place really turn me off. The latest one I heard is to give people the *what* but not the *how*. I know how frustrated I felt listening to that business coach's webinar and experiencing that technique firsthand. They are evil alien tactics to me. I have a hard time listening to webinars now because they all seem to follow the same formula, which goes something like this:

I was down in the dumps with nothing and nothing to look forward to until I suddenly realized what I needed to do to help myself and humankind in general. I pulled myself up by my bootstraps and made six figures that first year! Now out of the goodness of my heart I'm sharing these techniques with you so that you can do the same. Here's the first one. If you would like the rest, I'll be your best friend today and practically give them to you for only $997 - but you have to act today!

And, of course, that first technique is something we probably already know or would easily figure out using common sense. I find these pitches to be a waste of time for me. I may be interested in learning more about what the guru has to offer, but not that way. I don't offer webinars because I don't like them, even if I were to take a different approach to them. Not that nobody else should. I've encouraged some of my clients to offer webinars because I thought it would be a great vehicle for them. It's just not my thing. I prefer to offer in-person workshops instead, chock full of valuable information, hypnosis and NLP exercises, etc., and make a online course version of it available for anyone interested to experience it whenever and wherever they please.

The whole pricing approach of creating a sense of urgency never works for me, either, even though every single person I know with a business background has strongly recommended those tactics to me. I've had some limited-time specials just to see if they would bring in new business. They haven't. When people decide to use my services, they don't really care about the cost. They like my package deals - 3 or 6 sessions paid in advance for a lower per-session cost - but I've never received any new business because of a sale or special. Not once. I maintain a simple pricing structure and no longer offer any additional specials. When I started my practice I chose the highest pricing that felt right to me, valuing my services, and I've stuck with it. There may come a day when I increase my prices, but I will not decrease them. That would be devaluing my services, and that does not appeal to potential clients.

Think about all I've mentioned in this chapter. It's basically equating professional development with marketing. You don't have to advertise to get noticed. In fact, advertising generally hasn't worked for me. I've taken advantage of free ads in coupon books, etc., given away prizes for charities, and I haven't received any business from any of it. Maybe it's because of my field. Hypnotherapists are, to some extent, in the business of helping people kick the mental monsters out of their closets. People want to get to know us first before getting personal. Putting out an ad with my logo, name and title does absolutely nothing to bring me business because it tells people nothing about me and does not create rapport or trust.

I was given lots of encouragement and information in hypnotherapy school about doing health fairs. I used to do art fairs and loved them, so I was all excited about doing health fairs. I got my space all planned out, had a great banner made, had giveaways and a free relaxation experience for everyone. I enjoyed talking with many people and making new professional connections (some of which wound up being helpful), but I received very little new business from health fairs. In fact, I believe I have only gained one new client from all of the health fairs I've done combined. That has been a real disappointment for me, but it is what it is. I still enjoy doing health fairs whenever I have some spare time (which hasn't happened in a long time, actually), but I certainly would not pay to participate in one.

There's one advertising approach with which I have had fantastic success, however. Groupon vouchers have brought me much business, and they don't cost a dime. You pay on the back end, of course, with a reduced session price, but the vast majority of clients I get from those vouchers stick around for at least several sessions. There is a very, very important trick to this approach, however, which I accidentally stumbled upon. Be the most expensive service provider in your field with a voucher in your area. I'm talking like twice as expensive as the other guys. Why? Because you only want people to purchase it if they are serious about making changes in their lives and will stick around for awhile to accomplish this - and then will recommend you to others. You don't want to attract the yahoos who just want to see if they can be hypnotized, or take advantage of your inexpensive service offering, after which you never see them again.

Why does this advertising work? Because it's not just a logo, name, title and clever tag line. To publish one of those voucher offers, you have to include information about your qualifications, your philosophy, what makes you different, client testimonials, etc. Someone sees your voucher and wonders why you're so much more expensive than the other similar service providers in the area - if you're more expensive, you must be better. She reads all about you, and if she resonates with your approach, she checks out your website (extension of your office, remember?). If she likes what she sees there, she calls with questions or flat out schedules an appointment (online scheduling is the greatest thing ever, by the way). It's free advertising that gets you in front of many of your ideal clients in an effective way. Many of my best clients have found me this way and have since referred others to me. It's a great way to let people know that you're out there and how you're different. Here again, you're educating, not selling.

A couple of well-heeled businesspeople told me once that I should deactivate my voucher offers because they might make me look desperate for business and turn people off. I took their advice and deactivated an Amazon Local voucher I had out there, but the Groupon voucher was just getting started and couldn't be canceled. That voucher went active a couple days later and brought me a couple grand in business right off the bat, after only selling one of them. People were seeing it, learning about me and making appointments, and even forgetting all about purchasing the voucher! So I reactivated the Amazon Local one and just let them both ride indefinitely as free advertising. When I talked with those same businesspeople later about my success with that method, they were interested to hear about my experience and actually made notes about it. I had taught them something!

The other trick to using Groupon vouchers is knowing when to stop them. I found myself booked 6-weeks out at one point, and my regular clients were a bit miffed that they couldn't get appointments. I had been thinking that the voucher would go away after a certain number were sold, but when I called to check on it they told me they had been adding 50 more every month! I had them stop the promotion immediately. I make $150 for a regular session but only $30 for a Groupon session. The following year I noticed that I had half the sessions I did the previous year but made three times as much money each month!

I'm always open to new ideas to try, and I'm always learning all I can from everyone, but now I understand that the common denominator in the methods that work for me, the ones that help me build trust and rapport, are the ones that educate (usually for free) rather than trying to get people to sign on the dotted line and input their credit card numbers. I get many offers to put ads in magazines, on fitness center and restaurant televisions and on golf course benches, but I only take advantage of the free options that include educating the public. I have spent zero money on advertising since starting my business. Zero. I have no marketing budget. I am consistently full (as I define full, which gives me time each day to work on my business, too, and have time to relax and enjoy life) and it's all been word-of-mouth, with some initial business from the vouchers.

Thankfully, educational opportunities are almost always free or even pay you money! I take advantage of any and all free and paid presentation opportunities that come my way. And if none are on the horizon, I make my own by having a workshop. I do two-hour workshops that cost attendees twenty-five dollars each, and sometimes longer, more expensive ones. One client asked me to offer my *Hypnosis for Stress Relief* workshop last December, because she felt she could really use it. I offered it on the fly with little time to get the word out. Only three people showed up. We had a great time, I made seventy-five bucks that night, and I wound up getting $750 in subsequent business as a result of it.

Whenever I make it my mission to listen to my clients and give them whatever education they would like, the money follows. This does not happen for me when money is the driving force. So whenever I have slow times, as we all inevitably do, I keep myself out of desperation mode and ground myself in the real reason I do this work - helping others as much as I can. I know now that for every not-so-good week there's a great week around the corner - as long as I keep myself grounded in my identity as an educator, not a salesperson. People can tell when you see them more as a wallet than as someone you want to help make even better.

CREATE A WORKSHOP

Create a short workshop, perhaps introducing attendees to your service, and schedule a date, time and place to hold it free for anyone interested. Make flyers, post online and tell everyone about it!

Workshop Name: _____

Date:_____ Time:_____

Location: _____

EXERCISE

What information, concepts, exercises, etc., would you most like to teach others? Make a list, exhaustive as possible, of all of the things you would like others to know about not only your service but anything else from which you believe they would benefit.

_____

_____

_____

_____

_____

_____

_____

_____

_____

_____

_____

_____

_____

_____

_____

_____

Now use these ideas as the basis for talks and workshops, putting them together in different ways to offer different experiences for attendees. Are there certain concepts and exercises that you think would work well together? There's talk or workshop number one! Notate different groupings here, as lists, mind maps, flow charts or however you choose to represent them. Overlap is fine and probably unavoidable - just make sure that attendees would learn some different things in each grouping. Circle the grouping you'd like to develop as your first or next workshop.

NOTES

NOTES

NOTES

NOTES

NOTES

Chapter 6
MY (ALMOST) FREE EMPLOYEE

One of the best education and marketing tools I believe you can have is an effective website. The key word here is "effective."

I've been building websites for the last twenty years or so, and I've actually been employed in tech support. I am not a techno-geek who loves playing with computer stuff, though, unfortunately. I enjoy it just enough to do my own online work in the easiest way possible, and I don't want to spend a lot of time doing it. Whether you do your own web work or hire someone to do it for you, there are some things you'll want to understand about it.

A website is not just an elaborate digital business card, as I've heard some people describe it. I see it as the embodiment of my business vision and an extension of my office that does a lot of work for me. Because I see it this way, I program it differently than I might otherwise. I find ways it can take time-consuming tasks off of my plate to free me up for more sessions and creative pursuits. It is my best friend in business.

One of my website's big jobs is educating people who visit. It goes a big step beyond that, too, by giving visitors a feel of who I am. I am casual and professional, smart and creative and dedicated to their success, and all of that and more comes across on my site. The words and the feel of the site combine to give visitors an experience of me. My website is many people's first impression of me.

Many people want to do all they can online these days, so I make this possible for them. They can learn all about me, read testimonials (a must for all service websites), hear interviews with me, find out what events I have coming up and register for them, see and purchase my products, get a free relaxation audio file and newsletter (all automated), schedule appointments and maintain their memberships (control appointments, payment information, etc.).

At first I had a website with a popular online free website service. I designed and built the site myself easily and quickly, and it looked great. I used some apps (add-ons) for additional functionality and it worked just fine. After I started getting more than a few clients, testimonials, products, etc., however, I realized that my platform wasn't scalable. I needed to switch to a more sophisticated website builder to grow with my business and save me increasing amounts of time and hassle. I moved to WordPress with a theme that I liked, keeping it simple. I integrated plugins, and I went with Pike 13 for online scheduling and MailChimp for email campaigns and communication automation, all of which work well together to do even more work for me and save me more time.

If you don't do your own website, this will all sound complicated, and it can be. If you aren't inclined to do your own website, don't let anyone talk you into doing it. Hire someone (or better yet, barter). It'll take them a lot less time and save you a lot of stress. Just don't think you have to go the expensive custom route. There are simpler ways that will save your web designer time and therefore save you money. Discuss this idea with anyone you think about having program your site for you, and make sure you have access to and ownership of the site (if applicable).

There are certain elements I want included in my website to serve my visitors. I want to give them all possible information so that they don't have to get in touch with me if they don't want to, which goes against advice from every business person I've talked to about it. I would like to invite you to think of it like an extension of your front office. If they come to your office, you want to give them everything they're looking for by coming to see you. Don't make people register or contact you to get information. It will just annoy them and you'll be seen as an evil alien who just wants their contact information to try to sell them stuff.

Give, give, give. It's okay to offer visitors something extra in exchange for their email address if you want to, though. It's a good idea to have such a "call to action" on your site. If someone is interested in what you have to offer and wants to be kept in the loop with regard to your activities and offerings, certainly let them opt in to receiving the latest information about your business, and give them a gift for their interest (not a coupon, a real gift). I give a free short relaxation audio file to everyone who signs up to receive my email updates.

GET THE LATEST NEWS AND A FREE RELAXATION AUDIO FILE

Get a mix of wellness and happiness insights to outsmart your brain and engage your creative intelligence to remove blocks to your success and growth. And to get you started on your self-healing journey, I'll give you a free hypnotic relaxation recording to help you reduce stress!

To that end, you'll want to set up autoresponders for communications so that you don't spend a ridiculous amount of time keeping people current. I couldn't believe how much time I was spending just adding clients to my email list. It's boring but necessary work that can be done automatically. Enter MailChimp. Use whatever email service you like, but use one. I like MailChimp because it's cute and funny (if I have to do something mundane, at least I can be amused a little while doing it) and it does a great job at everything I need it to do - easily and for cheap. I design great looking email campaigns with it to automatically send whenever I want, and I use it to automatically add people to my list who opt in on my website. It also integrates with my appointment scheduling program, so that all new clients automatically receive a welcome email and free relaxation audio file before they even have their first appointment. They get a cool little gift that they almost always use and enjoy, and they can get used to my voice a bit prior to our first session so they feel more comfortable and have a better first session. Win-win.

My clients love, love, love online scheduling. There are always a couple who only want to schedule on the phone with me, but almost everyone prefers to schedule online. It's just so much easier and faster for everyone involved, and it shows that I am modern and progressive in my approach to business. There are many scheduling programs out there, so I had to do my homework. As I do both sessions and classes, I went with a solution that puts equal importance on both. The first program I used focused on appointments and worked with classes as an afterthought, and I had problems with it as a result. Pike 13, integrates with MailChimp, which is huge for me, and their support is fantastic. It sends appointment confirmations as well as reminders the day prior, which my clients really appreciate. It also integrates with my personal calendar so it's easy to keep all of my activities organized.

My point here is that if you see your website as your employee, you can reap huge rewards from it. Just make sure you build a site that will grow with your business. As your business vision comes into focus, design your website to handle the big picture. See it as an integral part of your business that does a lot of the busywork for you - marketing, email, data entry, appointment scheduling, etc. - and you'll get a lot more out of it than if you just think of it as an online business card.

PUT YOUR WEBSITE TO WORK

Find a job you currently do that you can program your website to do for you, then make it happen.

Job: _____

One final note about websites. At first I believed that no clients would find me by searching general terms online, so spending time and/or money on search engine optimization (SEO) would not pay off. I was wrong. Within about six months people started finding me through search engine searches, which made me realize that if I put a bit of time into SEO I could get more clients finding me. Not only am I on the first page for a Google search of hypnotherapists in my city, I'm *number one* in their business listing on that first page.

I did a few things to get it there. I used a domain that has had an active website attached to it for probably about 20 years and I bought a couple domains with "hypnotherapy" and my city name in it and pointed it to my site. I update my site content often (this gives me the biggest payoff), and I have a blog attached to it, to which I add a post about once a month at best (not as often as I probably should, but it seems to be working for me), all of which makes search engines like my site. I also added a WordPress plug-in to help me with SEO for every one of my web pages. I only optimized a few of the pages, but it was enough and it was easy to do.

I'm very happy with my placement in searches, and more and more clients find me that way now. So don't discount SEO. Spend a bit (not a lot, but a bit) of time and/or money making sure you get on that first page of Google for your area, and if you hire someone to make and maintain your website, make sure they can help you with SEO, as well. It's just another way to get in front of people who may be looking for you.

EXERCISE

Catch some epic internet waves. Do some surfing and see what functionality is offered by different websites out there. Like the online booking system on a counselor's website? Did you sign up for a coach's newsletter and receive a series of emails that you thought would be cool for you to send out, as well? Make a list of all of the "jobs" websites can do that you would like to find out more about and perhaps add to your site.

_____

_____

_____

_____

_____

_____

_____

_____

_____

_____

_____

_____

_____

_____

_____

NOTES

NOTES

NOTES

NOTES

Chapter 7
STICK THAT NECK OUT

It was hard to feel like an expert when I had just begun working in my field, but compared to the rest of the world, I was. So are you. So I have to show the world that I am an expert and own it - and so do you.

The marketing gurus all told me to make myself look like an expert in my field by publishing books, videos, etc. As it turns out, I've been wanting to write a few books for decades now. My hypnotherapy experience has been the missing piece for me, the part that brings all of my ideas together and completes my philosophy. What I didn't realize was how much personal and professional growth I would get out of writing a book, even a really short one. You learn a lot about yourself when you write a book.

I wanted to have some way of helping my clients continue on with their self-improvement after releasing what doesn't serve them, which we do in sessions, through the other three steps of my *release-grow-create-inspire* system that I think brings us true happiness, so I decided to write a book about it. In doing so, I got a much better feel for what my philosophy really was, polished it up, and understood how I have grown because of diving into and further refining it.

Then I realized that I didn't want people to just take in my ideas and think, "Okay, that's interesting," and put the book on a shelf to collect dust. I wanted them to take action and really get something out of it immediately. So I decided to make it a journal, instead - a one-month workbook to make a habit of paying attention to the ways in which you move through those four steps in your life everyday, to live in the moment, to be mindful. I wanted to give people a way to keep track of what's going on in their lives and realize how much they enjoy some of it as well as decide how they might want to change some of it to live the happiest lives possible.

This was a huge step for me in several ways. I was finally writing a book, but it wasn't much of a book - only ten pages of writing from me (which took me 20 years to write!) but lots of writing for the reader to do. I wanted it to be a meaningful personal results-oriented journey for the reader. I looked at all of the journals available out there, and I decided that the most suitable and cost-effective route would be to self-publish (I use CreateSpace and make all of my publications available on Amazon.com). I wanted it to be very affordable for anyone and everyone and get the most exposure.

I figured I wouldn't get rich on it, and that wasn't the point. I wanted it to be easy for people to use and enjoy. And they couldn't enjoy it until it was available, so I realized that I couldn't wait until I had a perfect version. I'll always see imperfections in my work, so I can't let that hold me back. I will not give in to paralysis by analysis. I had to just get the best version I could out there and let it fly (after getting feedback from a few folks first, of course).

Putting my ideas out there like that felt like I was sticking my neck out and inviting people to chop my head off. It was unnerving and scary. What if nobody liked it? What if nobody bought it? I think it only has one review (thanks, Dad!), but I don't care. It's out there and people can use it and hopefully be helped by it. That's all that matters. If it takes off and winds up on *Oprah's Favorite Things*, that would be awesome, but that's not the point. I'm very proud of myself for taking that leap, and everything else is a little less scary now. It's a great confidence builder to put yourself out there to be skewered and live to tell the tale. And every item you put out there is there for good - a permanent, passive income producer. That book has helped many of my clients, which makes it worth it right there. Now I have published three books and have more on my roadmap. It's fun and rewarding for me. Every once in awhile I sell one and I have a few extra bucks to pack up the dogs and head to Dutch Bros for a keto cold brew. Life is good.

The thing is, once you get really excited about your work and your message, you want to tell everyone about it, yell it from the rooftops. Because of this, I've sold many copies of my journal to people from networking meetings, as well as to clients. The best thing you can do for your professional development, your reputation and your business, in my opinion, is to let your passion run wild and come up with creative ways of getting your message out there into the world. Don't worry about what anyone else is doing. Do your thing your way and let it ride with pride. You'll get feedback that leads you to another creative idea, and another, and another. Your growth and development will show to the world that you are a professional driven to do all you can to help others. Every success is a real confidence-booster and every failure is a learning experience that will make the next project better.

I felt so good about publishing my journal that I published a Kindle version. Then I had a DVD made of one of my workshops and am now making them interactive online classes. I listened to my clients' feedback about the journal and published a companion online *21-Day Mindfulness Challenge* to give them journaling ideas and then, again at a client's request, made it an app for iPhone and Android (which is now defunct, but it was kinda cool for awhile to see people all over the world enjoying it). All of that led to *Mindful Thought and Activity Cards*, which wound up being bought by Amazon a couple of years ago and have been selling well ever since. I just produced some mindfulness cards for kids to get them started on a stress reducing and happiness enhancing habit for life, and I have a half dozen CDs available to help with various health conditions.

I've done a few interviews, all of which are online for all to experience. There is a video of me giving a guest lecture for a college psychology department lecture series for a couple hundred people. I have done ladies' nights with my yoga instructor friend, great workshops with a coach friend, a talk at a women's health symposium organized by a colleague and referral source - there's always a new opportunity coming up courtesy of someone else I've met. Every one of these public engagements has been a direct result of networking and making great connections with wonderful professionals in other fields. Be open to collaboration and you'll find yourself with many fun projects that broaden your horizons and your audience.

Do as many interviews as you can. You can even apply to be interviewed with some radio shows and online talk shows. You can spread the word about your business and have a really good time doing it! Good interviewers make it so easy for you. They know exactly what to ask and how to direct the conversation so that you can stay in educating mode (not sales mode) and get people really interested in learning more about you.

Clients let me know that they listen to my interviews and take note of my presentations and publications on my website before they make appointments to come see me. Different people are impressed by different things, so having a myriad of professional activities available to them shows potential clients that I am active in my field and gives them confidence in my dedication, enthusiasm and knowledge.

And the best part is that I'm having so much fun! When you love what you do, you enjoy sharing it with others. It's really fun to work with other professionals, too, to put on events that are different than anything I'd be able to come up with on my own. Those events expand my horizons because I learn from the professionals with whom I team up. They get in front of my people and I get in front of their people - now many more people know about me, recommended by someone they already know and trust.

Another way to expand your horizons is by attending professional conferences. I feel that the best thing these organizations can give me is professional development, through meeting others in my field and learning as much as I can from them. I believe in going to any conferences, workshops and seminars that sound fun and enlightening and in belonging to whatever organizations further my education and skill set.

Find and register for a professional conference that sounds fun and informative to you.

Conference: _____

Dates: _____

Location: _____

EXERCISE

Take a look at the workshop ideas you came up with in Chapter 5. How might you transform or combine them to get publishing credits and improve your credibility and expertise in your own unique little corner of your field?

Once you have the content figured out and organized for a workshop or talk, you can write a script for it and record it as an audio or video file (or CD or DVD). That script can also be the basis for a "special report" to give as a free gift for people who sign up for your newsletter or to sell.

Put all of your workshop groupings in different orders and see how the best fit together to tell one big story. Now you have the outline for a book! The script you write for each workshop ⟩ becomes a chapter in your book, which you can edit to knit together nicely with the other chapters (other workshop scripts) to give your readers the big picture of what you would like to teach them.

The point is to get your message out there to the public. Potential clients will see that you're a published author and you'll get instant credibility. You'll also get to pass on your knowledge and expertise and just maybe make the world a little bit better place. Always a good thing.

NOTES

NOTES

NOTES

NOTES

Chapter 8
WHAT'S MY WHY?

I've heard many business gurus talk about "knowing your *why*" and how important it is for powering your business. But not until Simon Sinek's TED talk on leadership did I understand how to utilize my *why* for maximum impact.

I've discussed focusing on my work, my professional development, having fun with inspired projects rather than focusing on making money, and how when I keep that focus I do well. Sinek's talk "How Great Leaders Inspire Action" explained why this works and how I should present myself and my business.

Sinek claims that the reason innovative companies and leaders are so successful is because they not only understand their *why*s, they present their products, services and ideas leading with their *why*s, then telling us *how* they achieve their *why*s, and then *what* they have available for us to experience their *why*s. Apple Computer is so successful, says Sinek, because they don't do what every other computer company does - showing us *what* product they have for us to buy, then telling us *how* they've made it so great and then asking for our money (which is ultimately their *why*). Apple takes the opposite approach. They tell us their *why*, that they believe in challenging the status quo, *how* they challenge the status quo is by making their products beautifully designed and user friendly, then showing us *what* they have for us to buy. They lead with their *why*, and by the time they tell us what they have for us we're reaching for our wallets.

Getting my business started, I was focused on *what* I did and *how* I did it. My *why* was there, but it was personal and private. It directed everything I did and the way I did it, but my focus was on letting people know *what* I did. I realized early on that everything I did in my business had to come back to my *why*, but not until I heard Sinek's talk did I realize I had to make my *why* public and use it as the driving force for my message, not just my work.

I had been telling people that I do hypnotherapy to teach people to get more control over their minds and bodies and remove any blocks that might be holding them back from living the lives they want. Nowhere in that description is my *why*. It was conceived and is driven by my *why*, but my *why* is not explicit in that statement. So I changed it around. I believe in truly empowering people to remove blocks and live the lives they want without reliance on external aids, and I do this by teaching them to have more control over their minds and bodies, for which I use hypnotherapy, coaching, NLP and guided imagery.

There are many professionals out there offering similar services and products to mine, so starting with the *what* doesn't inspire people, especially if your *why* is just making money. People buy your *why*, so lead with it.

Determine your why, how and what:

Why: _____

How: _____

What: _____

Here's your new purpose statement!

Presenting my purpose statement this way changes the way people see me as a professional. I am not just another hypnotherapist. I am someone who empowers people, who teaches them how to do for themselves. I use hypnotherapy, but I use other techniques, as well. I see myself as a teacher who uses hypnotherapy, NLP, guided imagery and coaching protocols as tools. All along I have viewed myself as someone who empowers others, but explicitly presenting myself to the world this way changes how others see me. I do more than just help people release blocks they've put on their progress. Throw a rock and you'll hit five life coaches who say the same thing. I help them get the most out of life that they can, living better, healthier, more productive lives - and, most importantly, I give them tools to do these things for themselves, without reliance on any more medications, therapies, treatments, etc., than are necessary. People don't typically think about all of this when they think of a hypnotherapist.

I always think back to what I heard at a business workshop one time: people want to hear about the fun they'll have on the tropical island, not the mechanics of the ship that will take them there. I no longer just give facts about what I do and how I do it; now I tell stories (with my clients' permission) that bring my *why* front and center, and people love hearing the stories and remember them because they resonate with them. They can be profound, amusing, wondrous, tug on heart strings, and they inspire listeners to empower themselves in the same ways.

The more I grow as a professional, the more I see that I am able to offer people. My expertise, knowledge and interests combine into a philosophy and practical system for life change that is a unique contribution. This is who I am as a professional. I empower people doing my thing, my way. When I go into a session in my office I don't think that my job is to just do hypnotherapy. My job is to help my client make the changes he wants to make and to give him tools to help him make more changes himself at home, and to grow into the life he wants with health and happiness and be an inspiration to others. That is empowerment, Amy style. That is my *why* in action.

In my book *Create Yourself: One-Month Journal* I present my idea that in any area of our lives we have to release what doesn't serve us, grow what does serve us, create new manifestations of that and inspire others to make their own unique contributions. The book you're reading now details my experience of applying this model to building my professional practice. I had to release negative emotion about money and business owner mentality and limiting beliefs about my entrepreneurial abilities. Only then could I really grow a business. I learned all I could about being a business owner and learned from every technique I tried, every success and every failure - every nut I gathered was examined, tasted and either kept or tossed. When I learned enough, I was able to create my own ways of doing things, from the system I use for sessions in my office to the unique workshops and talks that I give. In sharing what I've learned and created with others, I inspire them to start down their own paths to growth, whether as business owners or in some other aspect of their lives. We are a social species, and inspiring others brings us happiness.

I published my journal as a tool to help people make mindful living a habit. We have to see what's really going on in our lives and understand how we feel about it to determine whether we want to grow it or change it. We have to get in touch with the 98+% of our brain activity that is not routinely available to our conscious minds, because that's where the truth lies. Our conscious minds do not care about truth, they just want to make us happy and have us focus on what will help us survive for another day.

Just focusing on my business, I have to release stress constantly to get in touch with this subconscious truth using self-hypnosis or some other form of relaxation, and in doing so I see and feel what things I want to grow and what I want to change and how to change them. I come up with new workshops and new products when I'm relaxed and focused inward. Would I have come up with these ideas without releasing the stress? Perhaps, perhaps not, and certainly not as quickly. That release lets me know what else I may want to release and it allows for innovative thought.

As I continue on this journey of growing my business, I will continue to grow as a person as I keep reaching out of my comfort zone, and I'll find new limiting beliefs to release so that I can grow more, create more new ideas and share them with others in different ways. And each step will grow not only my business, but my happiness, as well. In this way, the Amy way, business growth is intertwined with personal growth. The concept of work-life balance becomes a rather moot point.

Why is it important for your business *why* to be so intimately associated with personal growth? Because if it isn't, you're basically left with "making money" as your business purpose. Making money does not equal happiness. There are many people with lots of money who are not happy, and there are many people who live in poverty but are happy. Money is a useful tool, with which we can generate things that make us happy, including having an ongoing hypnotherapy practice or any other operation that helps others. Money is a tool, not a purpose. I see money as the fuel that not only keeps my operation running, but allows it to grow so that I can increase and enrich my offerings. This is a very different view than providing my offerings for the purpose of making money.

Simon Sinek has a great example for this point in his TED talk. We all know that the Wright brothers and their team were the first to accomplish manned flight. What we might not know is that they had no money other than what they could squeeze from their bicycle shop, and they had not a single college degree among them. No reporters paid any attention to them. They were not working for money or fame. They had a vision that manned flight was possible and would change the course of human history, and they put all of their effort and passion into making it happen.

Conversely, Samuel Pierpont Langley had $50,000 from the War Department to pursue manned flight (a LOT of money in those days!). He held a seat at Harvard and worked at the Smithsonian and hired the best minds of the day. He had the support of the New York Times and the entire country. He also had a purpose - to be rich and famous. And his team worked with him for the money, not the dream. The day the Wright brothers took flight, Langley quit. He was not excited about a change in human history, of which he could be an influential part. Rather, he was not going to get rich and famous for being the first one to figure it out, so he lost his purpose. What if he had succeeded in achieving flight before the Wright brothers? He would have achieved his *why*. What then? Nothing. Game over either way.

I've thought about this often, and it's an enlightening musing. What if money was my *why* and I made all the money I wanted? What would I do with it? I'd make some changes, certainly, but I'm still the same person. I don't want to waste it, I want to do something meaningful with it. So after taking a few vacations, I would use it to grow my business, increasing what I can offer others and providing free help to more people that couldn't otherwise afford it. Following this line of thought, I've imagined what my business might look like, and I have some exciting ideas. I can see my business as a well-funded cash cow that uses the money to help more people in more ways. Again, I come back to my *why*. Money doesn't fulfill my dream, but empowering people does.

I would argue that money doesn't fulfill anyone's dream; to the contrary, it ends dreams if it's the purpose (you reach it and you're done or you don't reach it and you give up) or it enables you to accomplish more and more in line with your dream that goes beyond money. Every time I empower someone, whether I'm paid or not, I feel fulfilled in my business. I would like to empower more people, so money is a necessary and wonderful tool (not an evil), but it's not a purpose, not a *why*. When I started my business I made a point of earmarking about ten percent of my sessions for people who really want to use my services but absolutely cannot afford to do so. I put the same enthusiasm into these sessions and get the same satisfaction from them as I do with paid sessions, and they remind me that what I do is not all about the money. Now that I offer products, I use them as an opportunity to help others through donation of a portion of the profits.

I often hear that anyone in business is in it to make money. I would argue that we are all in business to help people, in our own special way, and if our offerings do indeed help people we will make money and stay in business, becoming more and more successful. The more we help people with more services, products, etc., the more money we will make and the more we can help others. Helping people is the *why*. Money follows and allows the *why* to be realized more and more if you do your job well and always put your clients first. Lose sight of your *why* and you lose sight of your business.

EXERCISE

Assume you have more money than you could ever spend. How would you change or grow your business? List these things and get a vision of your business at its peak. What is your purpose, the common denominator for the changes and growth? Does it align with your purpose statement that you created earlier in this chapter?

_____

_____

_____

_____

_____

_____

_____

_____

_____

_____

_____

_____

_____

_____

_____

NOTES

NOTES

NOTES

NOTES

NOTES

Chapter 9
LIFE AFTER YEAR ONE

You've made it through your first year as an entrepreneur. Congratulations! What's in store for you now?

One of the best things about making it through the first year is that your stress level starts to go down a bit, and not just because you get comfortable and confident with your purpose and with the new identity you've created as a professional. When I went through my fist year I had a stressful time with the slow months because I was always worried that I wouldn't get any more clients. I understood the concept of patterns of business, but that first year everything is emotional. Only in the second year can we begin to get a good feel for what our patterns of business really are. I had downer months and I had kick-ass months. I was better able to predict the course of the roller coaster, so I didn't stress out so much over the lean months because I knew that fat ones were on the horizon.

Bookings and income increase overall, too, during that second year, which feels awesome. I just wanted to stick my head out the window and yell, "I am a contender!" It hit me that I was making a living income with my practice and, contrary to the fears of the first year, it was increasing nicely.

I believe the trick is to set your prices as high as you feel comfortable and not run specials other than Groupon vouchers. None of this "One time only: buy one session, get one free! Hurry, sale ends at midnight!" stuff. It's not about getting as many clients in the door as possible as quickly as possible. I know a very successful long-time hypnotherapist who started off doing many sessions a day as the cheapest hypnotherapist in town and his car was repossessed shortly thereafter. He was working like crazy and not making any real money. Not to mention, you need lots of time - much more than you might think - to work on your business and nurture your creative projects. Remember, you have two equally important but distinct jobs: service provider and business owner.

Constantly re-evaluate your business processes. Is there something you could do differently or automate to save time? I realized that I had trouble seeing and reading the words on my file folder tabs because I had been taking them to and from work in a soft-sided hobo bag. For the first time in 20 years, I broke down and bought a briefcase that had a compartment for files to keep the tabs from getting bent. I just made sure my briefcase was bright orange to suit my personality rather than the typical "professional" black, brown or burgundy. Even little things like this impact your productivity. The bigger things have a bigger impact, of course. When I formed a new partnership with Amazon.com to sell my *Mindful Thought and Activity Cards*, I had to change how and when I ordered supplies and reorganize my home office to have space for them and enough inventory to fill Amazon's monthly order without delay, so that they had plenty in their distribution center at all times.

I realized early on that I had to set a limit to the number of sessions I booked each day. More than three in a day drained my energy and I didn't get anything else done except a few maintenance tasks like going through my emails and returning calls. I prefer to book fewer sessions per day and have time for fun, creative projects like writing a new book or meeting with referral partners to get joint workshops and other ventures going, all of which build my reputation as an expert and generate more business. Find your sweet spot and set up your processes, whether automated or manual - and stick to it. You can always make an exception, but you won't have to worry about having days when you're mobbed.

I set up my calendar so that all possible networking meetings I might go to (about a dozen or so per week) are recurring events on my calendar, but I'm seen as "free" by my online scheduling program. When I look at my schedule for a day, I see what sessions I have scheduled and if there isn't a session during a time I could go have a meeting with possible referral sources and clients, I go to the meeting. I stay pretty full with sessions, but every so often someone has to cancel and I have free time to go chat with other business owners. It's important to have frequent time with your professional support network, and I love the camaraderie. I usually wind up attending one or two networking meetings each week. Very few merit blocking out my booking calendar - perhaps one or two each month.

Clients always come first. Just don't bend over backwards for them too much - it's actually counterproductive. You look more successful if you aren't available at the spur of the moment. When someone has to wait a week or two for an appointment, they see you as being worth it. Right now you might be thinking, "Jeez, I just want to get as many clients in as possible!" I get it. I've been there. And I'm here to tell you that if you adopt the policies of a successful practice, not one that's desperate for clients, the public will see you as a successful practitioner and they will even more attracted to working with you. Whenever you feel desperation, turn it into respect and admiration for what you're building and the professional you already are. Be proud, and put yourself out there in a proud way. Just don't get cocky!

You also might want to establish strict business hours and not communicate with any clients or business associates outside of them. There's always a client or two who wants you at their beck and call. If someone calls me at 8:00 at night, I'll call them back the next business day during business hours as soon as it's convenient for me to do so. I wouldn't expect to get my doctor on the line outside of her business hours (or even during, actually, but you get my point). It was really hard at first for me to stick to this delay, but it really paid off. The ultra high-maintenance clients went away and I had time off from my business to chill out and reboot. You teach your clients how to treat you, so teach them to treat you with professional respect.

I've heard and read many successful hypnotherapists discuss starting up their businesses and how their practices grew. They all say that it takes several years to get to the point where you're consistently booked and you don't even have to think about marketing. Your practice is all word-of-mouth and referrals and you can raise your prices. Put in the work starting day one (or even before), and you'll see your practice start to move in this direction in the first year. My second year I was pretty much booked all the time and I started looking forward to those days when I'd get a cancellation or just not have anyone booked so that I could switch gears, chill out and work on one of the many projects I had on my roadmap.

After that first year I started to realize deep inside that I had a real, viable business. I didn't stress as much about possibly not making the money I needed each month and focused more on my purpose, where I saw my business going in the future. I saw four viable divisions: private sessions, online product sales, workshops and speaking engagements, and a mentoring/internship program. As I got more and more excited about these divisions, they took shape more and more and started to materialize.

Feeling and being seen as more established, I always have new opportunities coming my way, and I make sure I'm always open to them and take advantage of them as fun and/or educational experiences. Very seldom does an opportunity not pay off in some way, whether immediately or sometime down the road. I just enjoy the events, whatever they are, and I focus on getting to know people and spreading the good word.

Now's the time you may have some extra money to put into marketing or society memberships or extra certifications. Just keep thinking about ROI (return on investment - put on your business-owner hat), and don't fall into the trap of having a few hundred extra bucks one month and thinking you should spend it on something to build your business. The first thing that money should be earmarked for is to counteract a deficit you may have the next month or so.

It's awesome to produce a new workshop DVD. Just keep in mind how many you'll have to sell to get back the $350 you spent on the first 100-item minimum order before you start actually making a profit from them. Don't think you have to have every website plugin to fully automate everything. That $200 per year you spend to have customers from your online store automatically added to your email list isn't a great investment until you start having enough online sales that you find yourself spending quite a bit of time manually entering those names.

And don't think you have to stay in the same networking, certification or other professional groups. I made a rule that I would not renew a membership to a group that did not give me a positive ROI - in dollars, not just experiences. Each year I switch things up a bit, leaving groups from which I have not profited and joining new groups that sound like they may give me interesting and promising new experiences and opportunities.

Another thing I noticed after the first year is that I was tired. Really tired. I went all-out for a year and needed a break. My boyfriend took me on a wonderful vacation to Jamaica for a week, during which I unplugged and did no work. Not only did I recharge my batteries (thank you, rum punch), but when I returned I found that my business had exploded. I had lots of 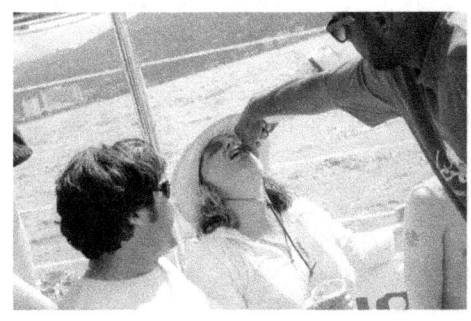 sessions scheduled, a radio show interview opportunity, a lecture request and more. That next month was my most profitable up to that date. We joked that we should take vacations more often! Seriously, though, make sure to disengage whenever you can to relax and enjoy all that life has to offer. It will make you more productive overall and attract more clients who want to be as happy and relaxed as you are. Remember: your mindset always comes across to others.

By the end of my second year, all months were comfortable. My first summer was slow, but my second one broke all to-date earnings records month after month. I was getting established. I was only going to one or two networking events each week and had increased my weekly session load. I was doing 10-15 sessions per week, every week, plus new client consultations, which I determined was my optimal session load. I could relax into my business and not try so hard to make it work, because *it was working*.

What's next? Growth. Continued growth as a professional and figuring out how much you want your business to grow. The more well-known you get, the more opportunities come your way. Your challenges will no longer be focused on getting business but on ensuring that the opportunities you take and the work you do promote your vision rather than splintering you in many directions and making you look confused rather than expert.

At one point in my second year I found myself in contract with a major hospital chain for sessions as well as the sales of some of my products. There was talk of a possible internship program down the road, which meant I needed to start entertaining the idea of hiring people or services to grow my business in ways I always saw it growing, just not so soon! Shortly after that two of my clients, who had such life-changing experiences that they wanted to become hypnotherapists themselves, asked if I would mentor them after they received their formal education. We are now in the middle of the first run of that mentoring program, and it's a fantastic experience that I want to expand.

I was comfortable seeing myself as a business owner in private practice, but becoming the head of a company (dare I say CEO? Yikes!) was a new level of professional growth that made my head explode with visions of evil aliens. I found myself back in *release* mode, ridding myself of the nervousness and cracks in my confidence. I spent quality time with successful corporate executives, finding support and mentoring that helped me formalize my business processes and grow personally to be able to successfully take on that next major professional challenge.

What will be your next major professional challenge? Well, if you focus on your purpose and let that lead your business, you'll keep going in that direction. If you find yourself heading in a direction that isn't much fun for you, make whatever changes are necessary to put yourself back on a course that is rewarding and fun for you and then continue to grow in that direction. Your vision can and should change as you grow and learn more about what is important to you. Goals should not be seen as things to accomplish, but rather as possible objectives to get you going in a certain direction which should change as you get closer and realize that you really want something a bit different. As long as you keep putting yourself out there, transparent and authentic and with enthusiasm, and you keep reaching for the big vision that you have for your business - what you *really* want - you'll keep moving toward it like a flower to the sun.

I would recommend letting the stress subside a bit first after the hairy first-year ride before getting more serious about the formalities of running your business, such as determining key performance indicators and such. Take a breather, then get more formal with your business when you have more time and attention to work *on* your business, not just *in* it. Learn from people who have been successful in businesses similar to yours, and who have grown in ways you want to grow. Just keep your business vision in mind.

Don't let anyone convince you that you have to grow toward being only the visionary only and hiring others to do all of the work. If this sounds good to you, go for it. Many of us who get into service-oriented work, though, do so because we find the *doing* of the work rewarding. I want to encourage you to grow your business in the direction of your happiness, not necessarily the direction that would be the most profitable. Keep your *why* front and center.

Grow as much and as fast as you are comfortable growing, always in the right direction for you, and remember that growth is one step toward creating and inspiring, which drive our happiness, which is (or should be) everyone's ultimate end game. Perhaps you want to wind up as the owner of a wellness center with many practitioners on your payroll. Alternatively, you may want to only do private sessions, and only a few per week. Either way, you will want to keep growing as an expert administrator and/or practitioner, and as you grow you will become more well known and in demand. Keep doing what's fun for you and let your business grow organically.

Consider not just whether to change the work you're doing in your business but also *how much* work you want to be doing. As you build your name and reputation, you can deactivate the Groupon vouchers and any package deals you may have. Then you can start increasing your prices. You may make enough doing three sessions per day, three days per week, along with CD and book sales to be making the money you want to make.

Include future planning in your business budget so that you save what you want to save for the future while enjoying what you want to enjoy of the present. Plan as much as you can with your long-term goals in mind, even when you're just trying to make ends meet.

Always remember that we get what we focus on. Whenever you find yourself thinking about limits (e.g., too few clients, too little income), force yourself out of that scarcity mindset and into an abundance mindset. Channel energy from negative emotions into positive actions toward what you want. Keep faith in yourself and in the path you have chosen.

EXERCISE

Start getting your finances in order, if you haven't already. See where your money is going and how much you want to be making to live comfortably. Set up some goals, short- (e.g., attending a conference or taking a vacation) and long-term (e.g., retirement), and add them to your budget. Determine how many hours you want to work to make what you want to make. Take all income sources (e.g., product sales) into consideration and decide how much you want to charge for your time. What changes would you like to start making to bring you closer to this comfort zone?

_____

_____

_____

_____

_____

_____

_____

_____

_____

_____

_____

_____

_____

NOTES

NOTES

NOTES

NOTES

Chapter 10
CELEBRATE EVERYTHING!

Be persistent with your positive attitude and actions and you will succeed in your own special way that is perfect for you.

Every step in a positive direction for your business is an event to be celebrated. Whether you've hit an income milestone or learned something not to do again, celebrate it in some way. Have tiny celebrations for small achievements and bigger celebrations for bigger accomplishments. Why? Because it feels good and keeps everything positive and exciting - even things you might otherwise see as failures.

Whenever I hit a monthly gross income record, I find a thirsty friend and we meet for a glass of wine and a nosh. That's not something I do every night, so it's special, but it won't break my budget. Go at happy hour when there's a deal on house wines and split a cheese plate or something. Good times!

I love clothes and add to my work wardrobe as a reward for slightly bigger accomplishments. I get some cool new threads to feel fresh and professional without going over the price limit I set for myself. Looking nice increases confidence and self-esteem, so it's the gift that keeps on giving. You might want to build up your work wardrobe little by little as you hit more and more records. Your closet feels better and better to look at as it becomes a testament to your growth and success.

I even celebrate the end of each work week by attending my friend's hot yoga class at her studio and going out with her and other yoga buddies for sushi afterwards. If I've had a particularly great week or survived a particularly challenging week, I might even get a pomegranate martini with my dragon roll. It feels wonderful to unwind both physically and psychologically at the end of the week. That doesn't mean I won't do any work over the weekend, but I won't have any sessions and can feel free to work on whatever floats my boat at home in my PJs with my dogs supervising.

During my whole first year (and most of my second) I worked all day, every day. Weekends were times for projects because I could really relax and totally get into the creative zone for as long as I wanted. These are great times, and this kind of work is very rewarding and promotes wellbeing and happiness. That said, we all need to take a day (or even - dare I say it? - two) off each week. Take a day trip, visit family, attend a beer festival or chili cook-off or some other fun day-long event, or just hang out with a friend at a pool for the day. Going to an event that aids your professional development or at which you find yourself networking is fabulous but not a day off. Feeding your soul will indirectly feed your business by continually enriching your life and making you feel fulfilled.

After all of the business promotion necessary when you first get going, as well as staying in front of people consistently, if less frequently, afterwards, it's easy to see everyone you meet as a potential client first and friend second. I met so many new people who became clients that I had to make a conscious effort to turn off education/consultation mode and get away from my business when I met new people. It's hard, because the first question everyone asks about you is your name and the second is your occupation. Even with established friends, one of the first questions we're asked is "How is work going?" Many people are intrigued by hypnotherapy and enjoy talking about it. I always answer their questions, but instead of letting my passion take over as I would in a professional mingling situation, I shift gears as quickly as possible to personal topics. This keeps me out of work mode and lets me enjoy getting to know people and interacting as friends.

You might consider seeing non work-related friendly gatherings as celebrations for staying in business. Value your time outside of your business. Don't feel like you can only allow yourself to spend the money to go to a museum if you make a couple of potential client contacts while you're there. By valuing your non work activities and being just a person, not a business owner, you decompress, enjoy more of life, and project the kind of person that your potential clients revere. You might find yourself getting clients from these events, too, even when you try not to! The carefree you who enjoys life and is always smiling will attract more clients than the business owner you who is always trying to sign people up for appointments.

Having my own business means I work more than my non business owner friends and make a ridiculously low dollar per hour (at least initially). The saving grace is that I'm doing what I love, which has huge payoffs when it comes to my happiness with life. Instead of thinking of work-life balance, I think of having regular non work time - a day each week, a couple of weeks each year - when I focus on other things, thereby enriching my knowledge, creativity, relationships and contentment. Had a really great year? Take a really great vacation! Didn't do so well? Take a less luxurious but still rewarding vacation. Visit a friend or relative. You'll come back refreshed with new ideas and a second wind.

Who are the most successful people in any profession? The ones who stick around. All businesses have highs and lows. It's our attitudes and actions that set the successful apart. Stay positive, have fun, celebrate everything, learn from what doesn't work and keep plugging away. Focus on what works and makes you feel good. By living authentically, doing your thing your way, you grow and succeed in ways that make you happy rather than trapping yourself in a professional mold to which you have difficulty relating.

EXERCISE

List ways you'll celebrate your successes, small and large. Include milestones such as hitting your maximum number of appointments for a day, week and month, highest earning day, week and month, giving your first workshop, coming up with a new product, even finishing the exercises in this book! Get used to celebrating your successes. Make it a habit.

Achievement   **Reward**

_____

_____

_____

_____

_____

_____

_____

_____

_____

_____

_____

_____

_____

_____

_____

NOTES

NOTES

NOTES

NOTES

Your purpose is your vehicle,
which is fueled by your passion.

Epilogue

At this point, you have created yourself as a business owner with your own unique brand. You are an original, and that's the draw that has clients filling your calendar, professionals asking you to give lectures and workshops and/or people purchasing your products. You've developed your own business processes that have brought your clients good results, and you're feeling more comfortable and expert every day. The exciting but stressful roller coaster ride has turned into more of an enjoyable, relaxing cruise punctuated by fun shore excursions.

Time to take off, silence any backseat drivers and keep moving forward. Enjoy the ride!

About the Author

Amy Rosner holds a Ph.D. in Experimental Psychology and spent 15 years teaching college Psychology classes and doing brain research, specializing in the neuroscience of visual attention and memory.

Amy combines hypnosis, guided imagery, neurolinguistic programming (NLP) and life coaching techniques to help people reprogram their brains, change their life stories and create new possibilities for success.

She lives with the love of her life and two wonderful dogs near Phoenix, AZ, where she was born and raised.

More information about Amy, her products and her services can be found at AmyRosner.com.

You can use the same system Amy used to build her business. *Create Yourself: One-Month Journal* is available at AmyRosner.com.

www.ingramcontent.com/pod-product-compliance
Lightning Source LLC
Chambersburg PA
CBHW051317220526
45468CB00004B/1378

* 9 7 8 1 7 2 1 2 1 5 6 5 2 *